WHAT OTHER

Nancy Beverly is a stellar storyteller! Over the years I have heard and read many stories from her life and ministry—always capturing the details with descriptive language, keeping you in suspense, making you feel like you were right there.

Her real-life stories make you hold your breath, anticipating good outcomes even as you fear otherwise. And every story compels you to see God, His care and compassion, His provision and protection, His precise intervention. Join Nancy and her faithful God in these adventures.
~ **Judy Douglass, Director Cru Global Women's Resources, Author and International Speaker**

Nancy Beverly has a powerful story, and I am thrilled she is publishing it. She has so many special experiences with God. Her writing style doesn't burden the reader to try and decipher what she meant; yet every story is catchy and makes me want to continue reading until I get to the end. There will be women in Eastern Europe who will benefit from reading this book!
~ **Tanya Onu, National Associate Leader in Global Church Movement, Moldova**

Very well done! I predict God will use this to encourage many.
~ **Dr. Charles Shepson, Founder of Fairhaven Ministries, Pastor, Speaker, Author of several books**

Nancy Beverly is a gifted storyteller who will captivate your attention with her incredible experiences in this inspiring collection of God-moments. God repeatedly shows up in the most surprising and unexpected ways.

This book is the perfect gift for anyone whose faith needs encouragement. After reading even a few of her stories, my faith was boosted to trust God more to show up in unmistakable ways in my life too. Tire Tracks is sure to increase your ability to believe that God cares about every detail of your life. Nothing is too hard for Him. Nothing!
~ Dena Yohe, Hope For Hurting Parents, Award-winning Author of "You Are Not Alone", Speaker and Mentor

Nancy's book is amazing and I thoroughly enjoyed reading it! I am so blessed by everything she shared. I think many lives will be touched by her incredible testimonies of God's faithfulness.
~ Linda La Scala, Psychologist and Homeschool mom

This book is the reason I stayed up until 5:00 am! I am hardly through the first 5 chapters and am enjoying it too much! Laughing, smiling, and many "oh wows." Nancy weaves Scripture through the stories in a way that is quite relevant to the challenges we all face in various stages of life. It is a terrific encouragement and balm for struggling hearts. I can't wait to see how God uses this book.
~ L. Chapman, Missionary, East Africa

I had so much fun reading Nancy's experiences as she trusts God. It made me think, "How do I see God working in my life?" Maggie Bruehl, Cru Staff Emeritus, Writing Coach,
~ Author of "Splash: Captured Moments in Time,"

Whether you are a skeptic or a Christ-follower this book is for you. You will enjoy, as I did, Nancy's honest and brave retelling of her encounters with God and His faithfulness to her. Learn and experience that God is love by reading Nancy's faith journey into heartache, healing, and joy.

~ Steven, Wycliffe Bible Translators

TIRE TRACKS

When God Unmistakably Shows Up

NANCY BEVERLY

Copyright ©2022 by Nancy Beverly.
All rights reserved.

No part of this publication may be reproduced, distributed, or transmitted in any form or by any means, or stored in a database or retrieval system, without prior written permission of the publisher.

Published by Bright Road Publishers.
Cover and design by Raney Day Creative, LLC.
Printed in the United States of America.

Scripture quotations marked NIV taken from the Holy Bible, NEW INTERNATIONAL VERSION®, NIV® Copyright © 1973, 1978, 1984, 2011 by Biblica, Inc.® Used by permission. All rights reserved worldwide.

Scripture quotations marked NASB taken from the New American Standard Bible Copyright © 1960, 1962, 1968, 1971, 1972, 1973, 1975, 1977, 1995 by The Lockman Foundation, La Habra, California. All rights reserved.

Scripture quotations marked NLT are taken from the Holy Bible, New Living Translation, copyright © 1996, 2004, 2007 by Tyndale House Foundation. Used by permission of Tyndale House Publishers, Inc., Carol Stream, Illinois 60188.

Scripture quotations marked MSG are taken from THE MESSAGE, copyright © 1993, 2002, 2018 by Eugene H. Peterson. Used by permission of NavPress, represented by Tyndale House Publishers. All rights reserved.

Have You Heard of the Four Spiritual Laws? written by Bill Bright, ©1965-2022 The Bright Media Foundation and Campus Crusade for Christ, Inc. All rights reserved. https://crustore.org/four-laws-english/ Included by permission

The names of some people and locations have been changed or omitted to protect the identities of individuals and mission work involved.

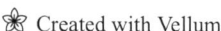 Created with Vellum

This book is dedicated to:

My children and their spouses, grandchildren, and future generations of the Beverly Family
"This will be written for the generation to come;
That a people yet to be created may praise the Lord."
Psalm 102:18

My husband Peter for his support and encouragement, and for playing a key role in many of these adventures

All those reading this who want to know if they can trust God with the things that matter to them the most. I was once where you are today!
"And you will seek Me and find Me, when you search for Me with all your heart."
Jeremiah 29:13

EXCLAMATION PROCLAMATION

I have been told by the grammar gurus of book writing that exclamation marks should be used sparingly—perhaps one or two in a whole book.

I must apologize that I have disregarded this venerable rule.

When the King of the universe steps out of the shadows and unleashes His love and power in a way so amazing no one else could possibly have done it, there's no other appropriate symbol than an exclamation! And in many cases, He deserves two or three!!

But I will stick to just one exclamation mark at a time, lest I be permanently excommunicated from the writer's guild.

So there you have it.

Consider yourself warned.

TABLE OF CONTENTS

Foreword
Tire Tracks!

Section 1 - U-Turn and the Early Road
Chapter 1 - Life from Loss 1
Chapter 2 - An Eye-Opening Water Hose 3
Chapter 3 - Second Thoughts 7
Chapter 4 - Clouds and Surrender 9
Chapter 5 - Uncrumpled 11
Chapter 6 - Transformation of the Tight-Fisted Tyrant 15
Chapter 7 - Will God Provide? 19
Chapter 8 - A Candy Store? No Way! 23
Chapter 9 - Advertising for A Husband 27
Chapter 10 - Early Morning Intrusion 31
Chapter 11 - Never Alone 35
Chapter 12 - When You Least Expect It 37
Chapter 13 - New Beginnings 41

Section 2 - Detours and Potholes
Chapter 14 - Humble Beginnings 45
Chapter 15 - Bills and Berries 49
Chapter 16 - Loneliness and Doubts 53
Chapter 17 - The Tire that Fell From Heaven 57
Chapter 18 - Stinky Socks and Runaway Mail 59
Chapter 19 - Sweet Sudie and My Peculiar Birthday 61
Chapter 20 - Waiting Again 65
Chapter 21 - Avalanche! 69
Chapter 22 - Desperate Prayer, Incredible Answer 73
Chapter 23 - Jesus Cares About Shower Curtains 77
Chapter 24 - Flat! 81
Chapter 25 - S'mores on the Dashboard 83
Chapter 26 - Tired of Trusting 85
Chapter 27 - Jesus Comes Through Again 89

Section 3 - Station Wagon Express
Chapter 28 - Creative Messes and Bedtime Prayers 95
Chapter 29 - Shelf on the Shelf 99
Chapter 30 - Spelling Bee Champ 101
Chapter 31 - A Big Fish Story 103
Chapter 32 - Bouncing Prayers to Heaven 105
Chapter 33 - Have Suitcase, Will Travel 107
Chapter 34 - Over the Cliff! 109
Chapter 35 - Last Call: Orlando 113
Chapter 36 - Standing—Literally—On the Promises of God 117
Chapter 37 - God Thinks Outside the Box 121
Chapter 38 - Now That's Customer Service 125
Chapter 39 - Desperate Cries 127
Chapter 40 - God's Face in the Wind 131

Section 4 - From Wheels to Wings
Chapter 41 - Stop That Plane 137
Chapter 42 - Look Out! 141
Chapter 43 - Storm of All Storms! 143
Chapter 44 - African Safari, Anyone? 147
Chapter 45 - Frozen in History 149
Chapter 46 - Broken Heart for the City 151
Chapter 47 - My Surprising Birthday Gift 155
Chapter 48 - An Unmistakable Answer 159
Chapter 49 - The Wonder of Bagels 163
Chapter 50 - Charging the Darkness 167

Section 5 - Final Destination
Chapter 51 - Lost Treasures 173
Chapter 52 - Tragedy on the Beach 177
Chapter 53 - Home! 183

Would You Like To Join the Journey? 185
Acknowledgments 199
About the Author 200

FOREWORD

My many years as a pastor have revealed to me that people have countless questions about God. If you were to ask me, what is the most commonly asked question, I would answer, "Is God good?" or, "Will God be good to me?" This question is often the question underlying so many other questions about God. I have found that for those who have trouble trusting God, it is this question and its answer that causes them to decide whether to place their trust in Christ.

The really good news is the fact God is aware of it. He realizes His goodness is often called into question. In fact, this suspicion was brought before Eve in the Garden: "Did God really say, 'You must not eat from any tree in the garden?'" Put another way, "If God were good, would He have restricted you from eating that fruit?"

People have been doubting God's goodness from the beginning of time and it continues today. We see the nation of Israel questioning His goodness throughout the pages of the Old Testament. God established annual holidays and a weekly Sabbath as a way of helping His people take time to recall His goodness while being renewed from the grind of life.

As we turn to the New Testament, we see the implementation of communion. The main point of communion is to "do this in remembrance of Me" (Jesus). It seems clear God wants to put His goodness on display in such a way that His people don't lose sight of it in the midst of the challenges of life.

As Lead Pastor of a local church, I lead a weekly staff meeting. With rare exception, it starts the same way every week, with the same question, "Who has a God-sighting to share?" In response, several will share tangible ways in which they experienced the goodness of God. I have emphasized with them it is very important to make note of God-sightings, because they are His goodness on display. Life is filled with challenges, and it is only human to sometimes wonder if God is present and aware of what we face. Taking time to consider His character and the goodness that flows from it is a true perspective-changer.

Why do I bring this up in the foreword for Nancy's book? I do so because her book answers this all-important question, "Is God good?" She provides a resounding answer, not in abstract theory, but from real-life experiences. I can tell you from my own life, once you resolve this foundational issue, many other questions will no longer call for an answer.

So if you have been searching for the truth in this area, come walk alongside Nancy in her faith journey as she discovers the answer is a resounding, YES, GOD IS GOOD!

Don Cousins
Lead Pastor Discovery Church
Orlando, Florida

TIRE TRACKS

Of course he sees me, I assured myself, as I glanced at the truck about to turn left. Prompted by the "walk" signal, I strolled into the intersection through the deepening shadows of dusk. Little did I know my leisurely walk home from work was about to become a race for my life!

Doubt replaced my confidence as I heard the truck's engine roar closer. I picked up the pace. Startled by approaching headlights, my feet pounded on the pavement as my heart pounded in my chest.

Louder and louder, faster and faster! Then I unmistakably felt something—or Someone—push my back forward just as the truck barreled by behind me. There was a woosh of air and a slight tug on the back of my sneaker.

Visibly shaken, I hobbled with jello-legs for the remaining five blocks home and tried to sort out what just happened. The explanation which made the most sense was that Someone shoved me out of the way just as the truck passed by. It was so close that its tire rubbed against my sneaker. There was a telltale black mark—a tire track—on the back edge of my shoe, which supported this conclusion.

It was alarming enough that I had almost started a new career as a truck's hood ornament. But more unnerving was, *Who pushed me out of the way?*

I was already deep in thought before crossing the intersection. The previous year I dropped out of college, planning to get married. Instead, I found the true Love of my Life, Jesus. *Now that I had decided to trust Jesus with everything, what was next?*

After this traumatic encounter, new questions flooded my mind. *What had God saved me for? What did He have ahead for me?* I didn't know the answers, but I felt His hand of protection and a new sense of destiny. I was overwhelmed with a profound realization that I am truly never alone.

As I look back on that event, I marvel at how it represents my walk with Jesus for the past 49 years. I could not have imagined the incredible life He had saved me for! And God never promised I wouldn't have troubles or close calls, but He did promise to always be with me. He has kept His promise.

This book records many times He has left unmistakable evidence of His protection and provision, like that tire track on the back of my shoe. My greatest desire is that these stories will inspire you to seek and trust the totally trustworthy God. He wants to leave His tire tracks in your life, too.

U-Turn and the Early Road

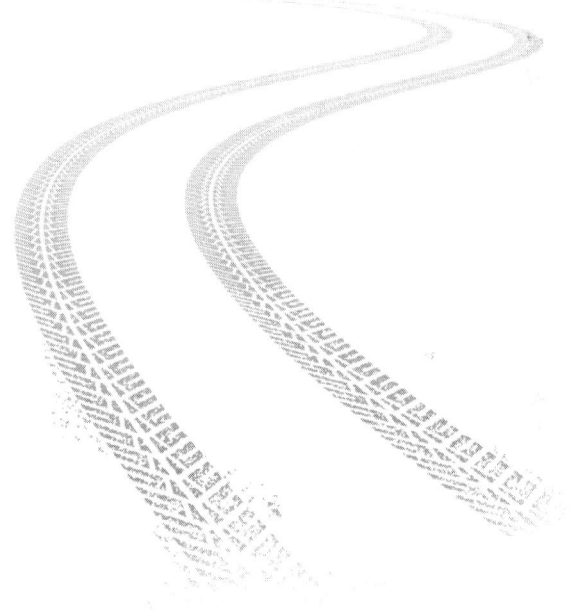

1
LIFE FROM LOSS

One thing my eighteen-year-old heart was convinced was unmistakably true: my whole world had just fallen apart. Two years earlier, I thought I had found the solution to the emptiness I felt inside. I longed for someone to love me and always be there for me, someone who would protect and provide for me. Like a non-swimmer flailing in a turbulent sea, I had tightly latched onto the first bobbing object floating close enough for me to grab: an equally messed-up guy.

Now, after dating Mike for a couple of years, my world was shaken by his announcement he was moving away with his family. *What about his promise to marry me, provide for me, have a happy family?* I couldn't see it, but he was just a drowning man looking for his own buoy to cling to, pulling me farther under with him.

I poured out my emotional pain by frantically sanding an old desk in the desolate darkness of my mom's basement. Streaming tears mingled with the sawdust as I slammed the sander back and forth, digging deep white grooves far into the wood grain. I felt so alone in my despair. I didn't know Someone was right there, weeping with me.

A few months later, I sat in the university cafeteria, writing yet another letter to Mike. Suddenly my solitude was interrupted by two friendly faces peering down at me.

"Hi, I'm Susie and this is Bonnie. Could you please give us your opinion on this little booklet?" As a lonely freshman, their friendliness was a welcome contrast to the huge impersonal campus. So I readily agreed. Bonnie later told me they had prayed God would lead them to the person He wanted them to talk to. And there I was.

As they explained how I could know Jesus and His perfect love, I noticed an unusual kindness and peace in them. I didn't fully understand their message, but I knew I wanted to know God. So I prayed to invite Jesus into my life, relieved to hear that once I invited Him in, He promised to never leave me.

Of all the students in that crowded cafeteria, why did they choose to approach me? Had a caring God seen my broken heart and sent two of His children to offer me a more trustworthy place to find love?

To reflect:
When have you lost hope in someone or something you were depending on?

To consider:
The Lord is close to the brokenhearted and saves those who are crushed in spirit. Psalm 34:18 NASB

What difference would it make during uncertain times if you knew someone who cares is with you?

2

AN EYE-OPENING WATER HOSE

I met Bonnie a few times that semester, and sat in on her small group Bible study. My ears perked up when they began talking about going to a spring break outreach in Florida. I was impressed that these Jesus-followers were doing exciting things and weren't ashamed to say His name in the crowded cafeteria without lowering their voices. Although I was attracted to their interesting lifestyle and the spiritual things they talked about, I was still tightly clinging to my boyfriend as my hope.

My big brother Gary felt I deserved someone better, so he introduced me to Ben, a family friend who had just come home from the military. I was surprised by how easy it was to quickly break up with Mike and begin dating Ben. I was so focused on finding someone to meet *my* needs and fill *my* emptiness, that it didn't matter who it was. But I soon discovered Ben's Prince Charming qualifications were lacking, too.

Over the next six months, I dropped out of college mid-semester rather than risk the trauma of possibly failing Biology and Chemistry. I started working at a yearbook company and became engaged to Ben, leaving Jesus and my new Christian friends far behind me. I even went so far as to reduce my definition of God to just a good cosmic force. This made it easier to not feel accountable to anyone.

But Jesus didn't give up on me.

One hot summer day, Ben was washing his car and squirted me with the hose. To even the score, I jokingly squirted him back. I was shocked when he angrily jumped in his car, screeched out of the driveway, and disappeared down the street. He didn't get in touch with me for three days.

It was like curtains in front of my eyes were suddenly opened, as I remembered my conversation with the two women in the college cafeteria six months earlier. Suddenly I understood what they were telling me.

I believed in God all my life, but now for the first time, I realized God was the only one who loved me the way I was longing to be loved. He was the only one who would never leave me, the only one always looking for what was best for me.

I was expecting Ben, an imperfect human being, to fill the empty hole in my heart that only God could fill. The physicist Blaise Pascal is credited with saying, "There is a God-shaped vacuum in the heart of each man which cannot be satisfied by any created thing but only by God the Creator, made known through Jesus Christ."

The selfishness I saw in Ben and in myself was part of what the Bible calls sin. The problem was, my sin separated me from God and His love. No matter how hard I tried, I could never be good enough to reach God.

This was where Jesus came in. God loved me enough to leave His perfect world, take on the form of a human being, and give His own life for me. If I trusted Jesus, He would forgive all my sins and I could experience the kind of love I had been searching for. His arms were stretched out wide to gather me in.

The next day I went to church for the first time in years. Sitting in the pew looking up at the cross, I gathered all the faith

I could muster and prayed a simple prayer. It was the best decision of my life. *God, if I can know you the way those two girls talked about, I'm interested. And if you have a better plan for my life, mine isn't working out so well.*

Ben eventually showed up again, as if nothing had ever happened. Outwardly things continued the same, but a longing for God's bottomless love had been planted in my heart. Digging through my old college calendar, I finally found Bonnie's phone number scribbled in the middle of some doodles. Picking up the phone, I made a call that opened the door to a life I never imagined possible.

A surprised Bonnie told me the new school year's Bible study started the following week. I made sure I was at that meeting—and every one after that. Each Tuesday evening was an oasis in the desert, the highlight of my week. I was anxious to find out what the next step in my faith journey was.

To reflect:
Where have you looked for love?

To consider:
I have loved you with an everlasting love; I have drawn you with unfailing kindness. Jeremiah 31:3 NIV

Have you ever looked to God for love? Why or why not?

3

SECOND THOUGHTS

I thought Bonnie would be impressed to see my beautiful engagement ring. Instead, she looked concerned. And to be honest, as I grew in my relationship with Jesus over the next few months, I also became increasingly troubled.

If I took knowing Jesus more seriously, it would pull me farther away from Ben. And if I drew closer to Ben, it would put distance between me and Jesus. It became more and more obvious as time went on that I couldn't have both.

The worst thing I could imagine was being alone. *What would Jesus do if I told Him He could do whatever He wanted to with my relationship with Ben? Did He know what was best for me? Could I really trust Him?*

As I read the Bible, I couldn't help but notice God's pure love and the sacrificial ways He proved Himself trustworthy. My Christian friends' lives were filled with joy and purpose, which I longed for myself. And I grew increasingly uncomfortable with some of the things in Ben's and my relationship which I knew didn't fit into Jesus' plan for my life.

Jesus would not push His way into my life; He waits until He is invited. I began to see when I invited Jesus into a specific area of my life, that area went so much smoother. Jesus began showing up right when I needed Him.

For example, one night I was driving alone through a dark, isolated area when my car stalled. Thankfully, it stopped right before a railroad track, not on it. But this was before cell phones so I was still in a bad situation, stuck alone in the dark.

Two things astonished me. First, an unexplainable peace and an awareness of God's presence washed over me instead of my usual fearful reaction. Second, in less than five minutes a police car that "just happened" to be doing his rounds drove up, pushed my broken car to the side of the road, and drove me safely home.

God was watching over me.

To reflect:
How would you describe your relationship with God?

To consider:
But God demonstrates His own love for us in this: while we were still sinners, Christ died for us. Romans 5:8 NIV

What does this verse tell you about God's love for you? What could you do to learn more about His love?

4

CLOUDS AND SURRENDER

My reluctant journey of faith took a leap forward when I attended a fall retreat with students from several different universities. It was such an encouragement to meet so many people my age who wanted to know Jesus better.

I admit I was hoping to meet a good-looking Christian guy. I'm ashamed I even took my engagement ring off. I did meet someone very special there, but it wasn't who I was expecting.

I can still remember the beautiful clouds billowing past the huge picture window as I sat in the retreat lodge, struggling with my reluctance to trust God with Ben. Searching my Bible for guidance, Romans 8:32 jumped out at me as if Jesus Himself was pointing it out:

"He who did not spare His own Son, but delivered Him up for us all, how will He not also with Him freely give us all things?" (NASB)

Why had I not noticed this before? I wondered. It spoke deeply to my fears.

Why would God lavish on me the exorbitant gift of His very own Son's life, then make my life miserable? If He loved me so much that He paid such a great price on my behalf, what He has in mind for my life must be very good, right?

So with the majesty of the heavens parading in front of my eyes, I finally decided I could surrender my love life to Him. *Jesus, I trust You with everything…even Ben.*

Two weeks after this huge step of faith, exactly what I feared happened. Ben broke up with me. I was surprised he had concluded I would be happier if I was free to pursue my new beliefs. But there was a bigger surprise: He was right. I felt unbelievably happy and tremendously relieved I was no longer being pulled in two opposite directions.

I had a few second thoughts in the months ahead, but there was no turning back. I was determined to settle for nothing less than God's best and I set my focus forward. God's Word became alive and I was excited to read it each morning, wondering what He would show me today.

I had incredible joy and peace, as I was free to go wherever Jesus wanted to take me.

To reflect:
What do you have a hard time trusting God with? Why?

To consider:
He who did not spare His own Son, but gave Him up for us all – how will He not also, along with Him, graciously give us all things? Romans 8:32 NIV

How could the truths in this verse make it easier for you to trust Him?

5

UNCRUMPLED

I ripped my "Florida or Bust!" sign off the cookie jar, crumpling it before slamming it into the garbage. That action accurately represented my inner distress.

As a fourteen-year-old growing up in Western New York, seeing Florida was one of my lifelong dreams. So when my older brother and his girlfriend invited me to tag along on a road trip south, I was ecstatic!

My mother, on the other hand, knew the reality of the situation. Exposure to alcohol and sleeping on the beach or in the car was hardly the way a young naive girl should discover Florida.

As I enthusiastically saved quarters and dimes in my "Florida or Bust" fund over the next few weeks, my mom said nothing. But when the day arrived, it was the only time I can ever remember her saying no.

Heartbroken and angry, I abandoned my precious wish. But God didn't. He tenderly tucked it away in a safe place, with plans to fulfill it in His way and in His time.

Fast forward about five years. Imagine how my ears perked up when the campus meeting announced their upcoming "Operation Sonshine" Christian outreach—in Daytona Beach, Florida.

So I rode 24 hours with a busload of enthusiastic, funny, spiritually-minded believers. I wanted to be like these college students who were free to have so much fun in ways that left them with a clear conscience. In God's loving wisdom, He knew these would be better circumstances than they would have been if I had gone as a fourteen-year-old.

I will confess, I was not as interested in sharing the Gospel as I was in finally seeing those ocean waves and palm trees. But Jesus had something even better in mind.

Deeply moved by a speaker's challenge to commit our lives to full-time Christian work, I stood with rubbery legs and agreed to pursue a path of service to Him. I had seen my life transformed and was beginning to see how I could be used to help others experience the same kind of new life. *What could be more meaningful and eternally significant?*

This dramatic commitment led me to return to college for a degree in Communication. Then I could work on a college campus sharing the message which had dramatically changed my life. God gave me my heart's desire, a trip to Florida, in His way and His timing.

In an ironic twist of events, the organization we work for moved to Florida. So we have lived in Florida for 18 of the past 28 years. I can imagine fourteen-year-old Nancy's eyes growing wide and her jaw dropping in astonishment, if I were able to tell her she would not only visit Florida someday, it would become her home! She might even dig the sign out of the garbage and tape it back on the cookie jar.

Like the Lord did, bringing my dream back to life.

To reflect:
What were your biggest disappointments, as you look back on your life?

To consider:
The Lord is my shepherd, I lack nothing. He makes me lie down in green pastures, He leads me beside quiet waters, He refreshes my soul. He guides me along the right paths for His name's sake. Psalm 23:1-3 NIV

What does this tell you about God? If you really believe this, how might you view your disappointments differently?

6

TRANSFORMATION OF THE TIGHT-FISTED TYRANT

Growing up, I viewed God as an "emergency hotline." I lived life as I pleased. Then when all else failed, I called on Him to change my circumstances. When the crisis passed, I quickly "hung up the phone" and went back to calling the shots.

But when I began to learn what the Bible says, I discovered Jesus wanted to be my best friend all the time, not just someone I called for emergencies. And He was far more interested in changing *me* than changing the circumstances around me.

I was surprised that living the Christian life involved both obedience and faith. When I read about something in the Bible that God was not pleased with, I needed to choose to obey what His Word says. But outward behavior and words were only the beginning.

I could never have victory over my sin just by cranking out external obedience. Jesus wanted me to admit my sin to Him, then surrender control of that area so He could transform me from the inside out. Changed actions were the result of a changed heart.

I immediately had the opportunity to test whether these truths worked: my sister and my priceless wardrobe.

Liz had this annoying habit of wanting to borrow my clothes. I had what I thought was a justifiable habit of making her squirm when she asked to wear anything in my half of the closet. I wanted her to grovel a little as one of my royal subjects to whom I was bequeathing a tremendous favor.

As I grew closer to Jesus, I disliked this harshness I saw inside of me. So Jesus and I had a little talk. Well, mostly I talked and He listened. *Lord, I confess my harshness toward Liz is wrong. Thank you for paying for this sin on the cross. I don't like being selfish with my clothes, but I can't change my heart! Will you please change my attitude toward Liz?*

It's not always this fast, but I was shocked that my miserly attitude melted away almost immediately. Within a day or two, it was completely gone! I still had to make the choice to share. But when Jesus changed me on the inside, I gladly lent her my clothes, with a genuine smile directly from my heart.

Liz is now one of my closest friends. I asked her recently—almost 50 years later—what changes she noticed in me after I believed in Jesus. Without a moment's hesitation, she replied, "You weren't selfish with your clothes anymore!" For a high schooler who loved looking fashionable (she's now a fashion engineer), it spoke her language of love. This played a part in her becoming a Christian several years later.

Living the Christian life in my own strength is more than difficult; it's impossible. Only Jesus can live the Christian life, so the only way I can live like Jesus is for His Spirit to live His life through me. Jesus is a gentleman and will only do this if I ask Him.

The most amazing miracles God performs are those He accomplishes in a Jesus-believer's heart when, little by little, He transforms them from the inside out. It's like a beautiful rose blossoming and losing its thorns. The same Spirit who raised

Jesus from the dead and holds the universe together lives inside everyone who invites Jesus into his life.

This truth has transformed my life.

To reflect:
What do you think people struggle inwardly with the most? What do you struggle with?

To consider:
But the fruit of the Spirit is love, joy, peace, patience, kindness, goodness, faithfulness, gentleness, and self-control. Galatians 5:22 NASB

Which of these qualities would you like more of in your life? According to the story, how could you experience it?

7
WILL GOD PROVIDE?

There I sat, on my mom's living room sofa. And sat. And sat. As I waited each day for what seemed like much longer than the one or two weeks it was, I questioned Jesus' goodness and power.

I had returned to college to get my degree, so I could then work full time at a university telling others about Jesus. Even though I needed to earn enough money for the next school year, I stepped out in faith and agreed to spend my summer at a Christian outreach project. But I was still sitting at home, packed and ready, and Jesus seemed uninterested in helping me get to the project.

My plan was to sell my engagement ring for bus fare from Buffalo to Hampton Beach, New Hampshire. After several responses to my ad, there were no takers. The project starting date came and went, but I had no Plan B. There was no one to talk to about this big test of my young faith, since there were no campus meetings or staff available during the summer months. So it was just Jesus, my Bible, and me.

"Be glad for all God is planning for you. Be patient in trouble and prayerful always." (Romans 12:12 Living Bible)

I hung onto these promises as an unsinkable lifeline in my stormy ocean of doubt. *Was I going to believe God had many good things planned for me that I could be glad for, when it seemed He was doing nothing? Could I be patient and wait and keep praying, as the verse said?*

Ultimately I chose to believe He was at work on my behalf, even though my circumstances seemed to say otherwise. And I waited. But I can't say there was much joy in the journey.

After a week or two of waiting, my older brother Jon felt sorry for me and lent me the bus money. I ecstatically boarded the bus. Many hours later, I was warmly welcomed by fifty other students and staff living in a big house two blocks from the beach.

Everyone on the project was required to work during the day, then we had Bible classes and outreaches in the evenings. My first big challenge was finding a job, since most businesses had already filled their summer positions. I had asked the Lord to help me with my sweet tooth over the summer and expected His answer would be a physically active job far from food, so I could lose a few pounds. But He apparently had a different idea.

I trudged from shop to shop and finally discovered a grocery store that had an opening...in the bakery. So I arranged brownies, cupcakes, and cookies in pretty rows, trying to ignore the crumbs. I enthusiastically sold those sugary delights to anyone who came near. Alas, this lasted for only three days. The owner realized that if he hired someone underage, he wouldn't have to pay minimum wage, so he let me go. Bye-bye, brownies.

The next day a woman came to our house desperate for someone to work at her takeout stand. Of course, I jumped at the chance. So off I went to this new assignment...where I swirled ice cream cones, whirled delicious milkshakes, and scooped tantalizing hot fudge onto sundaes. Three days after starting here, all the money disappeared from the cash register. I should mention, the cash drawer latch was broken. So it just hung open, a temptation to anyone who passed by. Rather than figure out who did it, she just fired everyone. See ya, sundaes.

The following three days, I canvassed almost the whole boardwalk and each rejection sent my spirits lower. Late the third night, I walked along the beach for a long time, and then quietly sat in the sand. I watched each white wave suddenly appear out of the darkness, explode with life and energy, then dissolve into the night. This was followed by a pause of inky blackness, broken by another white wave. This pattern repeated itself over and over again.

As I poured out my heart to my Heavenly Father, in the listening stillness it occurred to me that the Lord's blessings are like these waves. His faithful provisions come as continuous and certain as the whitecaps. But like the ocean, there are times in life between the waves when we don't see anything except the black night. During those times, we must place our faith in the certainty that another wave is coming and will break through the darkness at any moment.

So I laid it all in His Hands and walked back with renewed hope.

To reflect:
Have you ever had to wait a long time for what you wanted to see happen? What, if anything, did you think about God during this time?

To consider:
All the paths of the Lord are lovingkindness and truth to those who keep His covenant and His testimonies. Psalm 25:10 NASB

What difference would it make if you knew that every moment you were waiting, God was thinking about you and constantly at work on your behalf?

8

A CANDY STORE? NO WAY!

No. *Not the candy store, Lord!* A crowd gathered in front of the shop's bay window to watch workers bag another batch of caramel corn. I had avoided the place, knowing that working there would plop me into a raging sugar inferno. But by now, I was desperate. And that is how I ended up becoming the chief saltwater taffy clerk at Junkins' Candy Shop.

For some reason, Mrs. Junkins liked me. You might even say I became her favorite. After all, I was the one she usually sent to pick up her Greek gyro sub for lunch. And she trusted me to help keep track of her financial records.

My job ended up being so much more than a weekly paycheck. Mrs. Junkins became somewhat of a grandmother to me, and she even invited me to live with her the next summer to be her personal assistant. Even though I declined this flattering offer, it symbolized the special bond we had both found that summer of '75. Two summers later I ended up back there, promoted to the fudge-cutting department.

A small, wiry woman well past the age when women usually retire, Mrs. Junkins had started the candy store way-back-when and was not about to surrender it to some young whippersnapper. Guessing her age was a common topic of discussion among the workers to fill the boredom during slow times. But it remained her little secret, along with her peanut butter fudge recipe. I'm guessing she was in her eighties, yet she had more energy than many of the high school students who worked for her. The main evidence of her age was her poor hearing, which led to a humorous interchange one day.

She asked me, with an affectionate smile, "Who sent you here?"

"God did," I replied. Between her poor hearing and her New England accent, she thought I said "The guard did."

"Let's send him a nice big box of saltwater taffy, to thank him," she exclaimed. I smiled, imagining the box of taffy flying upward. *It would need to be sent by airmail,* I chuckled to myself.

I learned a great deal that summer about expectations. My biggest expectations for the project were that I would grow closer to Jesus and would share Him with others. I did indeed mature in my faith, but I didn't expect so much of it would be through challenges. I also enjoyed spiritual conversations with beachgoers, but the most meaningful discussions were with some of the candy clerks. One trusted Jesus to come into her life.

I expected to save enough money for my college expenses, which included my unsuccessful plan to sell my engagement ring in May. As things were winding up for the summer, I was surprised when someone who had inquired about the ring three months earlier called me out of the blue to buy it. The delay in selling it gave me time to struggle with my doubts. I learned to cling to God's trustworthiness, rather than my interpretation of what was happening. This deepened my faith roots and showed me firsthand, "He is a rewarder of those who diligently seek Him" (Hebrews 11:6 NIV)

I expected God to give me a job far from sweet temptations.

Sometimes He allows us to be face-to-face with our enemy so we can depend on Him and learn new coping strategies. Fortunately, taffy isn't my favorite, so as I headed back to Buffalo, I felt I had faced temptation rather than run away from it.

As I look back at these expectations for that summer, I am amazed at how the Lord fulfilled every single one of them—but not at all how I anticipated. I learned that His ways are higher than my ways, and when my plans aren't falling into place as I had imagined, I can still trust who He is more than my circumstances.

To reflect:
Have you ever had things look hopeless right before something really good happened? Can you describe what happened?

To consider:
Mightier than the thunder of the great waters, mightier than the breakers of the sea— the LORD on high is mighty. Psalms 93:4 NIV

What does this picture of God's power say to you in your circumstances today? Are you willing to trust them in God's hands? Why or why not?

9

ADVERTISING FOR A HUSBAND

I stared way up at this tall, handsome freshman as he enthusiastically exclaimed, "I just want to tell people about Jesus!" We were both waiting for a bus to the same dorm complex, and discovered we were "neighbors." Peter had become a Christian over the summer and joined our first gathering of the school year when he saw a poster. It said, "Wanted: Christians for Fellowship! Come to our Meeting!"

That year, a group of friends who lived in our complex hung out together. Peter was shy, but it amused me as he came alive when our group went square dancing. He had such a big smile while doing the hokey pokey, and waving his long arms over his already-tall body made him so much taller. My heart did a few flip-flops when he held my hand during the doh-see-doh.

By now I realized that in past dating relationships, I had been searching for someone to fill the God-shaped vacuum in my heart. Someone who would meet *my* needs. Now that Jesus was filling His rightful spot, I was not so empty and needy. I still longed for someone like-minded to walk through life with me; but in the meantime, I really enjoyed helping others know Jesus.

The following school year, a few of us began praying

together on weekday mornings. During these prayer times, my heart was hopelessly captured by Peter's pure heart and sincere faith. He didn't want a fancy car, wealth, or a prestigious career. His main goals in life were to know and love Jesus and help others know Him. Those were mine, too!

I confided in my small group leader about the struggle of being attracted to someone three years younger than me. Pris told me with a discerning smile that she was three years older than her husband.

After that, it seemed suspiciously like the work of a matchmaker when Peter and I were assigned to be co-leaders of our group's publicity. Our height difference made us the perfect team for the task because Peter, being tall, could tape the top corners of our advertising posters. Being a foot shorter, I could tape the low corners. Often we would celebrate our accomplishment with a soda.

Finally, our first date: a double date to see Fantasia, with ice cream afterward. Soon we were studying together and spending most of our free time together, and I never got tired of being with him.

We did silly things, like squeezing each other's hands at each landing as we walked down a flight of stairs. Holding hands, sitting close, and short goodnight hugs and kisses were as far as we went before marriage, which built my respect and trust. We jokingly called each other Chester and Martha, hiding our teeth and talking like elderly people.

Peter would often be waiting after my evening class with a strawberry yogurt, and he always opened doors like a gentleman. And how we loved to pray together! On one 24-hour bus trip to the Daytona Beach Spring break outreach, we sat together and prayed individually for each of the 50 people on the bus. Prayer continues to be a powerful part of our lives.

I watched Peter grow into a humble but strong leader and was proud to see him taking steps of faith—like being part of our group's central leadership team and teaching weekly classes and discussion groups. He was well-liked and became known for his frequent puns and signature exclamation, "BAY bee!" I was his biggest cheerleader and imagined how I could help him accomplish God's calling for his life.

Several months after we met, we made a startling realization: I was the one who made and hung the poster which brought Peter to the gathering at the beginning of the school year. You might even say I unknowingly advertised for my husband!

To reflect:
What would you want to know about God in order to trust him with your relationships, especially romantic ones?

To consider:
No good thing does He withhold from those who walk uprightly. Psalm 84:11 NASB

What kind of God does this verse describe? What relationships could you trust Him with?

10

EARLY MORNING INTRUSION

I was jolted wide awake by a man's muffled voice and the jiggling of the fire escape door handle a few feet from my bed. "Oh, it's locked," he mumbled in hush tones to his partner.

There were about 50 students and staff on my summer project, with women's bedrooms on the second floor and men's on the first floor. My room was the last one, right next to the fire escape. Earlier that week, I was alarmed to discover that women had been regularly enjoying personal devotions on the platform outside the door, then forgetting to lock it when they came in. If an intruder came up the fire escape stairs and opened the emergency exit, my unsuspecting sleeping head would be the first thing he would see.

So I immediately posted a reminder, "Please Lock the Door." And it was a good thing I did! Only two nights later, these uninvited guests showed up. The women across the hall also heard the men outside and closed their door. When I heard their door click shut, I thought the men had gotten in and were holding my neighbors captive. Heart pumping wildly, I stumbled down the hall for help. Meanwhile, the women across the hall heard my footsteps and assumed the guys had gotten in and were running down the corridor.

So I paused with a half-whisper at different rooms, making my way downstairs to the men's hallway door. Barely peaking my head in, I squeaked out a pathetic, "Help! Help!" Thankfully, this got the attention of someone with incredibly good hearing. He roused the whole first floor, and soon there was a stampede of men charging down the women's hallway to rescue the damsels in distress. The prowlers had left the fire escape long before, thankfully, and the women across the hall were shaken up but safe.

This traumatic event, which took years to recover from, was a great example of the all-knowing and unfailing protection of God. However, I couldn't escape from replaying over and over again in my mind what *could* have happened instead of what *did* happen. *What if I had not noticed the unlocked door? What if I had not bothered to post the reminder? What if the men had planned their dark intrusion three days earlier?*

For months, even years, I locked and blockaded doors at night and triple-checked windows, much to my various roommates' dismay. Clouded by my fears, I robbed myself of the peace I would have had if I had grasped God was in control of everything all along. Trauma counseling was not common back then, but over time the reality of Jesus' presence overshadowed my fears.

It is comforting to know I didn't have to feel the reality of His truths in order for them to be true. His protection was always right there.

To reflect:
Have you experienced something traumatic which left you feeling afraid? If so, can you share what happened?

To consider:
The Lord is my rock, my fortress, and my Savior; my God is my rock, in whom I find protection. He is my shield, the power that saves me, and my place of safety. Psalm 18:2 NLT

What does this verse say about God? What would it look like to trust a God like this with your safety?

11

NEVER ALONE

I wasn't expecting that phone call.

As I stood in the crowded kitchen of the summer project house, Peter's familiar voice on the other end explained, "After talking with Jack, the staff guy on my summer project, I realize I'm not ready to pursue a serious relationship. So I think it's best if we stop dating so I can focus on maturing as a man and growing closer to Jesus."

By now, I was thoroughly convinced that Jesus needed to be in the center of any dating relationship. I had told Jesus that if Peter was not His choice for me, or Peter was the right choice but it wasn't the right time, then I trusted His leading.

I was surprised by the total peace after the phone call and in the days that followed. It assured me that I had not grabbed my relationship with Peter back from Jesus' hands. I was truly believing "No good thing does He withhold from those who walk uprightly." (Psalm 84:11 NASB) If Peter was a good thing for me, we would eventually get back together. Unlike in earlier relationships, I truly wanted what was best for Peter—even if that wasn't me.

We avoided each other the following school year, which was

hard since we still lived in the same dorm and were both student leaders on the ministry planning team. The few times we did stop and talk briefly, it amazed me how he was learning the same things spiritually that I was. But I didn't want to get distracted unless he would consider me as more than a friend. It was my senior year, and I anticipated the excitement of doing what I loved most—helping people know Jesus—as my full-time job.

That year was a time of realizing how the Lord had taken my shallow, self-focused heart and was gradually filling it with His unselfish love. My fear of being alone was blanketed over by a sense of His presence. Jesus was first in my life, and by now I had learned He was worthy of my trust.

I knew I would never be alone again. Jesus was always with me.

To reflect:
Do you fear being alone? Can you describe a time when you felt alone?

To consider:
The Lord Himself goes before you and will be with you; He will never leave you or forsake you. Do not be afraid; do not be discouraged. Deuteronomy 31:8 NIV

What does this verse tell you about God? If you really believed Jesus will never leave you, what difference would it make in your attitude toward life and the choices you make?

12

WHEN YOU LEAST EXPECT IT

With college graduation on the horizon, I was thrilled to receive my long-awaited acceptance to work in campus ministry. The training was a great time of graduate-level Bible classes, ministry training, making new friends….and getting to know one old friend again. Peter happened to be at staff training, helping with childcare. I remember a few humorous times together which felt like a date but the stated purpose was to talk about why we couldn't date.

For example, once we went canoeing at the nearby park where he was full of puns, as usual. I laughed hysterically when he said, "I canoe all things through Christ who strengthens me," his version of "I can do all things through Christ who strengthens me." (Philippians 4:13 NASB) I went back to my room and sighed. I dated others, but the comparison only showed me there was no one I enjoyed being with like Peter.

I was assigned to Chico State University, California. You could not get much farther from Buffalo, New York, which made Peter assess the situation more seriously. Before I could report to my assignment, my next task was to discover a team of partners willing to invest financially in my ministry. This took several months, during which Peter and I began spending time together again.

I will not jump to conclusions, I told myself. *I will consider him a friend—just a friend—while I'm here for a few more months...unless he clearly tells me otherwise.*

At last, the day arrived when my team of financial partners was complete and I could report to my assignment. The week before I boarded a plane for California, Peter invited me to dinner at a fancy restaurant. As they seated us next to a beautiful waterfall, I observed, *how thoughtful of Peter to arrange such a fancy celebration of my accomplishment.*

I was completely caught off guard by what happened next. Reading the Bible passage in Genesis chapter 3 about how it's not good for man to be alone, he asked me to marry him! *Did I hear that correctly?* Speechless, I nodded my head yes! After discussing our future together, we were embarrassed to discover the restaurant had closed an hour earlier but they didn't want to disturb us.

We announced our engagement that weekend at the fall retreat. It was in the same conference center where I had looked out the big picture window and surrendered my love life to Jesus five years earlier. Jesus had certainly proven Himself to be faithful. He took Ben away so He could give me His best choice for me, in His way and His time.

We had a long-distance engagement while I ministered in California and Peter finished his senior year in Buffalo. I admit I was distracted from the work I had looked forward to doing, and floated on cloud nine after Peter's phone calls. I am thankful we spent so many hours writing to each other, because those written pages are a treasure. Recently we re-read one love letter each evening, reliving our early hopes and dreams and the love for Jesus Christ interwoven in every letter.

To reflect:
Do you think trusting Jesus' plan instead of your own is a good idea? Why or why not?

To consider:
The Lord will accomplish what concerns you. Psalm 84:11 NASB

In this story, how did God finish something that concerned me? What would you like to ask Him to finish in your life?

13

NEW BEGINNINGS

We had a simple wedding seven months later. Since this was before the internet, online websites, and cell phones with free long-distance calls, there was no way I could plan a wedding in Buffalo from California. But our Sunday School teacher's wife, Alta, agreed to be our wedding coordinator. She did a wonderful job and I didn't have to worry about anything except getting myself ready.

The service and reception were a joyful blur that flew past too quickly. At last, we were Mr. and Mrs. Peter Beverly! After being pelted with rice, we cruised along in our big brown Buick LeSabre—God's provision just in time for our wedding. As we popped the wedding audio cassette into the tape player on the way to our honeymoon, I was especially curious about one part of the pastor's message. Listening to it again, we hear him state, "Nancy, there will be times you will disagree with Peter. And Peter, there will be times Nancy will disagree with you." So both times I was the one disagreeing!

While my parents couldn't provide a fancy wedding, my heavenly Father was able to provide beyond what we imagined. My sister Liz is an excellent seamstress and made a beautiful wedding dress on a shoestring budget. A friend of a friend had an uncle who offered free use of a honeymoon cabin, tucked away in the beauty of the Adirondack Mountains.

The week we needed to pay for our wedding cake, which was $100, we got a check from Peter's grandparents for $107. They had even thought of the tax involved. It was lilac season, and a church member donated flowers to decorate the reception hall, filling it with sweet perfume. College friends did beautiful performances of the songs we chose: "God Gave a Woman to Me," "My Tribute," and a medley of "Father, We Adore You" and "When I Survey the Wondrous Cross."

These special memories took place almost 43 years ago. Our early idealism about marriage has collided with reality over the years, but Jesus has remained our unchanging anchor through life's storms. Today Peter and I can honestly say we enjoy being together more than when we were first married and are more in love than the day we said, "I do!" Jesus has made all the difference.

I can't begin to imagine what I would have missed if I had insisted on choosing my life partner without waiting on Jesus.

To reflect:
What good things are in your life? List them.

To consider:
Every good and perfect gift is from above, coming down from the Father of the heavenly lights, who does not change like shifting shadows. James 1:17 NIV

Have you ever considered that every good thing has been given to you by God? What does that tell you about what He is like?

Detours and Potholes

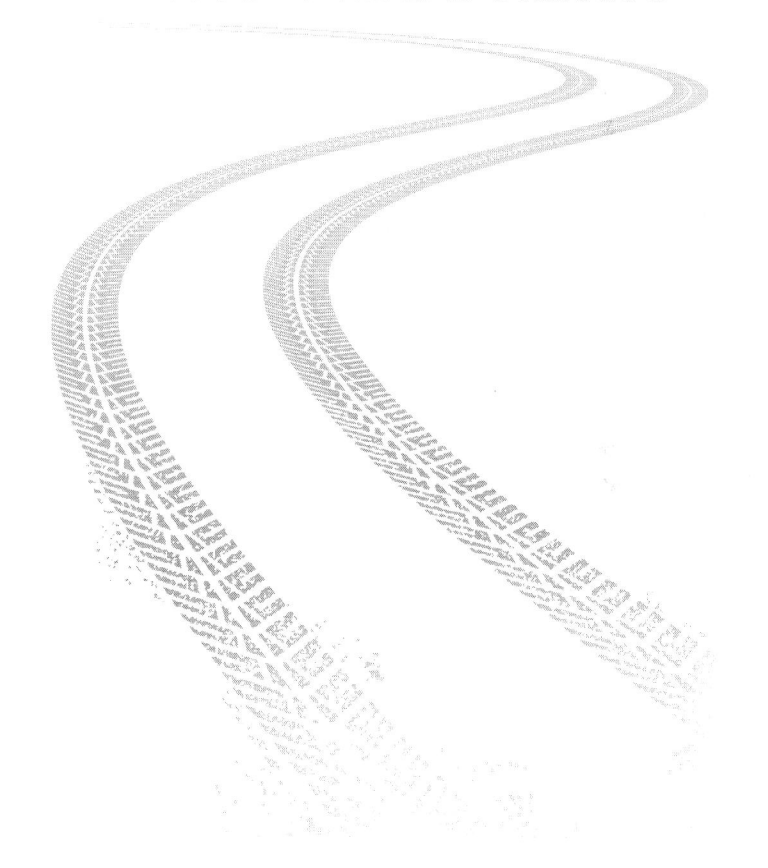

14

HUMBLE BEGINNINGS

It was the worst possible way to celebrate New Year's Eve.

The rain beating down on the tin roof of the small, old trailer sounded like an army doing target practice. I stared at the sliding closet doors which didn't slide, and the drawers which hung crookedly in their place.

The feeble space heater offered little to ward off the shivering cold which sunk deep into my bones. We had left our winter coats in New York, because we foolishly assumed South Carolina resembled the tour books year-round, with swimsuit-clad tourists sunning themselves on the beach. All we had seen was freezing, pouring rain.

I tried not to consider how the narrow hallway would now be our eighteen-month-old daughter's bedroom. But I was absolutely crushed, and tears silently slipped down my cheeks as Peter moved boxes into our new home.

Convinced this was the Lord's timing for Peter to begin graduate school, we had sold most of our furniture and vacated our huge apartment in Buffalo. This ancient mobile home was the only place we could find near the seminary which fit our budget.

After two days of disheartening attempts to cram our possessions into the tiny nooks and crannies, we decided to escape claustrophobia by exploring the area. About 100 meters past the school, we noticed a big sign: Apartments for Rent.

We inquired, and an older lady showed us her very best duplex, one of 13 apartments and mobile homes set back among the trees. This place was just beautiful, and much of what I had prayed for. The rooms were huge, especially after squeezing into that closet-on-wheels.

For some reason, Louise really wanted us there, so she lowered her rent by almost $100 a month to make it possible. We transferred our boxes into our new home the next day.

I was astounded to discover it was partially furnished and contained exactly what we needed, but nothing extra. It was like God's hands had brought pieces of a puzzle together.

We had brought a kitchen set, and there was no kitchen set. We had sold our dressers and bed, and there were two dressers and a double bed. We had brought nothing for the living room, and the living room was full. The end tables even had rounded corners, so our toddler would be protected. And there was a small table and a chair for Peter to use as his desk. God had thought of everything.

Let the classes begin!

To reflect:
If this housing provision and perfect match of furniture were God at work, what does this tell you about what He is like?

To consider:
But seek first His kingdom and His righteousness, and all these things will be given to you as well. Matthew 6:33 NIV

What would it look like for you to seek His Kingdom and His righteousness first? What are the "all these things" that sometimes take too much priority? Can you trust Him to provide them for you?

15

BILLS AND BERRIES

The apartment was great in many ways, but we did not lack opportunities to trust God. Although Peter found temporary jobs here and there, the economy was not good and our unpaid bills piled up. One time we added up our stack of bills and they totaled $360. This was an overwhelming amount of money at the time.

"Why don't we take a minute and ask God to send us $360 to pay them off?" I suggested. So we prayed, then moved on to projects that needed attention.

A few weeks later, we received a call from Nina, an old college roommate, and her husband Forrest. Phone calls were expensive back then, so we wondered what the occasion was. I had written to her and mentioned in passing we were under financial pressure, but nothing specific.

Forrest said they wanted to send us some money, and apologized that it was an odd amount... $360! Julia began running around the house, excitedly shouting, "Meerchil! Meerchil!", her two-year-old version of "Miracle! Miracle!"

We learned God answers specifics when we pray specifics.

Then the end of the first quarter came and tuition was due for the second quarter. I was hurrying to leave for a women's Bible study, so we offered up a very quick prayer. We asked for tuition money, if God wanted Peter to continue his seminary studies. Then I dashed out the door.

The next thing I knew, Peter was excitedly knocking on the Bible group door. I couldn't believe he held a big wad of money someone had anonymously put in our school mailbox. It was marked "for tuition" and added up to $660, the exact amount we needed! We had not planned ahead for our expenses very well, but God hears the cries of His children.

God is interested in big things like $660 tuition bills, and He's also interested in the small things. It was the week of our anniversary, and I told the Lord I wanted to make Peter a red raspberry pie, his favorite. However, money was extra tight that week and I couldn't even afford our basic necessities. So I scrounged around in the university's emergency food pantry, where students left miscellaneous items they didn't need.

What do you think someone left in the pantry? You guessed it: a large jar of red raspberries! I never saw berries in the food pantry before or after, so it certainly seemed like it was a special birthday gift from a loving Father.

There's nothing too big for Him to handle. And there's nothing too small for Him to care about.

Peter received his raspberry pie, and God received the glory!

To reflect:
What is your favorite part of this chapter?

To consider:
"I am the Lord, the God of all mankind. Is anything too hard for me?" Jeremiah 32:27 NIV

If there's no concern too small for God to care about and nothing too big for Him to handle, what would you like to talk to Him about today?

16

LONELINESS AND DOUBTS

At the time, living in a duplex surrounded by woods seemed more like a prison sentence than a gift from God. *Please, Lord! I beg you, can you please provide for Peter to finish school?*

However, after Peter's first year of seminary, there were no more miraculous provisions for schooling. For the next two and a half years, each time a new quarter of school was approaching, I would pray and plead with God to enable Peter to go full-time. But nothing.

So Peter worked full time and took one class at a time, paying his tuition through ordinary means such as Christmas gift money, savings bonds, or tax returns. I realized later that it is also God at work when our needs are met through unremarkable, everyday things.

I grieved what I had left behind in Buffalo. It felt like almost everything I depended on had been pulled out from under me—friends, family, money, ministry.

Shortly after we moved into the duplex, we discovered we were living in a "ghost town." Of the 13 units in the housing complex, only four of them were occupied. At times I experienced deep loneliness, as I traded living on the edge of a big city surrounded by people and stores, for being surrounded by…pine trees and bugs. I went from walking daily in our busy neighborhood, to having to restrict myself to our yard since we were advised it wasn't safe to walk alone on the road nearby.

I went from leading our women's Bible study at church to a city where there seemed to be a hundred Christians per square foot. With so many students from the seminary, I felt certain there was nothing I could contribute.

Spending time with Jesus put things in perspective. He showed me that His ministry could go on fine without me at center stage, and I needed some humbling. I began to see I was more motivated to help others when I received people's praise, but serving Him in the privacy of my home was just as significant to Him, if not more so.

I also realized I often determined my self-worth based on what I did and what others thought of me, instead of how my Creator saw me. Jesus wanted to tell me, "Nancy, even if you never tell another person about me, never lead another Bible study, never do another act of kindness, you are very, very precious to me. I love you so much I died for you. *You are mine!*"

As time went on, I believed His truths more and more, not just in my head but in my heart as well.

To reflect:
Can you relate to any of my struggles in this chapter? If so, which one?

To consider:
Praise be to the God and Father of our Lord Jesus Christ, who has blessed us in the heavenly realms with every spiritual

blessing in Christ. For He chose us in Him before the creation of the world to be holy and blameless in his sight. Ephesians 1:3,4 NIV

According to this verse, what is it that determines your self-worth? How could believing this truth affect your everyday life?

17

THE TIRE THAT FELL FROM HEAVEN

"Lord, can you please provide a used E78-14 tire at the flea market today for a ridiculously low price?" we prayed that morning.

One of our tires was quite bald, and there was no way we could afford a tire unless God came through. After our expectant prayer, we eagerly looked for the answer at several flea markets. We were disappointed when there was not one single tire for sale, let alone our unusual size.

Afterwards, Peter dropped me off at a coffee shop to have a couple of hours to myself, and took our two young children to a nearby park. While pushing them on the swings, he happened to look up past the playground. There, way out in the field behind them, were a bunch of tires lined up. The high school football players ran through them as part of their warm-ups.

Curious, he walked over to look at them more closely. *Not an impressive lot,* he thought, as he examined the row of old, beat-up tires. He did a double-take, though, when he got to the last one. It looked practically brand new!

Can you guess what size it was? Yes, an E78-14 tire! The coach gladly exchanged our old bald tire for this almost new one.

When Peter told the gas station attendant across the street how we got the tire, he exclaimed, "You got yourself a *good deal!*" and changed it for free.

If we had found a tire at the flea market, we probably would have given God the credit. But isn't it so unmistakably God, when He answers in a totally unexpected way?

To Reflect:
If you were God, how would you have answered this prayer?

To Consider:
Which of you, if your son asks for bread, will give him a stone? Or if he asks for a fish, will give him a snake? If you, then, though you are evil, know how to give good gifts to your children, how much more will your Father in heaven give good gifts to those who ask Him! Matthew 7:9-11 NIV

What do these verses tell you about God's attitude toward you when you ask Him for something?

18

STINKY SOCKS AND RUNAWAY MAIL

As the satirical poet Lord Byron once said, "Truth is stranger than fiction."

It also can be funnier.

We had one enormous mailbox for everyone who lived in the complex, so we had to sort through all the mail to find ours. If expected mail didn't show up, we would ask to check our landlady's coffee table. Stacks of peppermint patties, bags of chips, and sodas toppling over resembled a refreshment stand. Buried haphazardly under the wrappers and opened cans was more mail —sometimes with our name on it. My long-lost photo order found its way to that table, along with a few letters from home which had mysteriously opened themselves.

One time the landlady's son-in-law went off his medication, so to escape his nightly pounding on our door, we slept at a friend's place. The next morning we discovered our home had been broken into. Nothing was stolen, but the intruder had discarded his smelly socks while sitting at Julia's little desk. Thankfully, he started his medicine again and things continued as before.

Two wild turkeys lived on the property and wandered freely,

sometimes giving us a not-so-friendly greeting at our front door. Seeing them hang upside down from a tree at night was quite alarming. One of them disappeared around Thanksgiving, so it probably ended up in someone's roaster instead.

Wednesdays were my big day out. I would drive Peter to work so I could have the car to go food shopping. I often had a hard time sleeping the night before because I was so excited about getting out to the grocery store and laundromat. I'm not sure if this is humorous or pathetic.

We could not make up some of the things we experienced during our seminary days. Perhaps it was preparing us for living in a different culture several years down the road.

To Reflect:
Is there something you can laugh at as you look back, that wasn't so funny at the time?

To Consider:
However, as it is written, what no eye has seen, what no ear has heard, and what no human mind has conceived, the things God has prepared for those who love Him. 1 Corinthians 2:9 NIV

What do you think God might be preparing you for, through your past and present experiences?

19

SWEET SUDIE AND MY PECULIAR BIRTHDAY

It was unlike any other birthday before or since.

The morning started out ordinary enough. We lived in a duplex surrounded by woods, so I pulled aside the bedroom window curtain expecting to enjoy the tall pine trees.

Instead of peaceful stillness, I was greeted by chaos. Several police cars and an ambulance were haphazardly parked, while policemen and medical personnel were frantically running around. My first thought was, *Oh, no! Sweet Sudie must have had a heart attack*!

Sudie was a fragile elderly woman who lived in the other half of our duplex with her adult son. She often brought us a big piece of her pound cake, explaining every time exactly how to beat the sugar and butter until it was completely fluffy, not grainy. Sudie gave our toddler Julia a baby doll for Christmas, thoughtfully searching for one to match our daughter's brown eyes.

I hurried outside to ask what happened. When a policeman finally paused long enough to explain, I struggled to grasp what he told me.

Sweet Sudie had shot—and killed—her son.

I was stunned. Her son Jack seemed down when we saw him a week earlier at a neighborhood barbecue in our backyard. If it had been just the three of us, we would have talked with him about how he could know God personally. But there were other neighbors around, so we gave him a booklet that explained how to experience God's love, and encouraged him to take it home and read it.

That was the last time we saw him.

My husband and I visited her in jail a couple of days later. There was sweet Sudie, dressed in an orange prison jumpsuit. Peering at us through the tiny visitor's slot, she explained what had happened.

"He had a drinkin' problem. I warned him to stop drinkin'… but he didn't listen. So I shot him in the shoulder, just to scare him. I didn't mean to kill him. The bullet bounced off his shoulder bone and went straight into his heart."

We shared with her about Jesus' forgiveness and prayed for her. A short time later, they transferred Sudie to another jail, so I'm not sure what happened to her. But I know what happened to me. This tragic event deeply impressed on me two important truths.

First, you never know the intense drama exploding behind the quiet doors you walk past in your neighborhood. Be kind, give the benefit of the doubt, share your chocolate chip cookies or chicken soup.

Secondly, you never know when today is the very last chance a person will have the opportunity to hear and receive God's gift of forgiveness and eternal life. It reminded me of the Bible verse in James 4:14. "Why, you do not even know what will happen tomorrow. What is your life? You are a mist that appears for a little while then vanishes." (NIV)

To Reflect:
What did you think of this story? What is your reaction?

To consider:
This is how much God loved the world: He gave His Son, His one and only Son. And this is why: so that no one need be destroyed; by believing in Him, anyone can have a whole and lasting life. John 3:16 MSG

If you haven't accepted God's gift of eternal life, would you like to? If you have already invited Jesus into your life, is there someone you want to share His great news with?

20

WAITING AGAIN

Tired. So tired, day in and day out. Physically drained, for sure, but the emotional and mental weariness of caring for young children was even more exhausting. I felt trapped in a never-ending whirlpool of trying to keep one step ahead of baby spit-up launched onto the carpet, roaches skittering in the cupboards, and fifty creative ways to cook rice and canned vegetables.

Caught up in my self-pity, I didn't usually notice the beautiful blue sky, the fresh smell of pine trees, and the crackling needles under my feet as I hurriedly hung another load of cloth diapers on the line. Even if we had been able to afford the marvelous new invention of disposable diapers, they had not yet discovered the necessity of elastic around the legs and waist. Disposables created a nightmare of their own.

We were thrilled to welcome our son Daniel's arrival. Our increased volume of laundry created a convincing argument for us to finally get our own washing machine. Laundromat excursions with little ones in tow were replaced by conversations with the clothesline.

After living in this housing complex for almost a year, we

found out it was on the school's "do not rent" list. This explained why it was almost empty. When the property came under new management, the school changed its status and the housing units quickly filled up with seminary students. Although we had amicable friendships with our neighbors, they were busy with classes and I continued to distance myself through negative self-talk.

Why would they want to know me? Could I risk letting them see the doubts and struggles I hid behind my surface smile? I convinced myself I must be inferior to those who could afford school full-time, an outsider looking in. So I continued to feel isolated, lonely, and useless at times.

Despite my self-doubts, God showed His love through this neighborhood of believers. One couple in the mobile home across from us stayed for only one semester. This was just long enough to answer our prayers for someone reliable to watch Julia while I was in labor, and bring her to the hospital afterwards. The husband actually worked next to the hospital so when we were ready for Julia to meet her little brother, it was the exact time for him to go to work. He didn't even have to make an extra trip. How's that for perfect timing?

As Daniel got older, a pediatrician and his wife moved in next door. The doctor treated Daniel's frequent ear infections for free, which was a great provision during this short period when we had no medical insurance.

One terrifying day, I was thankful our neighbors were around. I turned my back in the yard for a second and Daniel, about 18 months old at the time, suddenly vanished. In a panic, Peter and I ran around the buildings calling his name. We searched up and down dirt driveways and combed the edge of the thick, foreboding woods and underbrush surrounding us. Nothing. Not a trace of Daniel.

My heart raced and prayers flew as Peter and I futilely searched for twenty minutes or so. Just as we paused to regroup and neighbors joined the search, who do you suppose nonchalantly toddled down one of the dirt pathways? We never did figure out where Daniel had been, but judging from his smile, he enjoyed his afternoon stroll. It was a relief to have friends join us in our frantic search, even though it appeared Jesus guided Daniel safely home without our help.

As is true for any of us, there were good days and bad days. But no matter how I felt, God's Word always stood solid underneath me as I clung to His truths. I had the choice to either believe Jesus was still good, loving, and all-powerful, as the Bible says, or to think He must not care since my circumstances seemed to say otherwise.

To reflect:
What kind of negative self-talk do you struggle with? What advice would you have given me at that time?

To consider:
But we have this treasure in jars of clay to show that this all-surpassing power is from God and not from us. 2 Corinthians 4:7 NIV

How could the truths in this verse be a helpful reminder if you are tempted to think you are inferior to others?

21

AVALANCHE!

Just as Jesus' crucifixion was followed by His resurrection, sometimes God's greatest sunrises come when things seem the darkest.

This was one of those times.

Three years after starting seminary, Peter was working full time and no longer taking classes. It felt like I would be hopelessly stuck for the rest of my life in the middle of those woods, with mosquitoes as neighbors. Overly dramatic, I know. But it seemed true at the time.

Then one Friday at 5:00 pm, Peter was told by his industrial parts company that his full-time job was being changed to part-time. At first, we assumed he would need to find another full-time job. Then we discovered the next quarter of school started in only four days and surprisingly, every class Peter needed to graduate was offered. It was not too late to register.

Could God be arranging things for Peter to finish his graduate degree after all? Was He answering my pleading prayers over the past three years?

One small problem...we had no money saved for tuition or living expenses. Something big would have to happen. Fast! I remember sitting in the school parking lot, praying with Peter that Jesus would make it clear what He wanted us to do. Some little birds circled and landed on our car. I wanted to believe it was the Lord reminding me of Matthew 6:26 NLT, " Look at the birds. They don't plant or harvest or store food in barns, for your heavenly Father feeds them. And aren't you far more valuable to him than they are? Just like I take care of these birds, I will provide for this." It seemed impossible that it could actually happen.

But God specializes in the impossible.

The avalanche of God's miraculous provision began when we asked a couple who had taken us under their wing, to pray with us. They responded by offering $1,000. We asked two churches to pray for us to know what to do, and they each initiated giving us a gift. Within the next 48 hours, we received an outpouring of unexpected and unasked-for gifts (including an anonymous $1,000 money order) as well as refunds we had been waiting months for.

By Monday morning, the Lord had brought in *all* the finances we needed for full-time school and living expenses for the whole quarter. On the first day of school, we were still saying, "What just happened?"

In May, we both gave great thanks to our mighty God as Peter walked down the graduation aisle. Shortly after that, we joined a Christian organization. When Peter received his new administrative assignment, it amazed me that the experience Peter gained through his jobs equipped him perfectly. What I thought was a delay in God's plan was the very thing that prepared Peter for his ministry.

God *had* heard my prayers and decided to answer them in a way in which Peter and I would grow the most, and He would receive all the glory. He completes what He begins in His way and His time.

To reflect:
What have you given up on?

To consider:
Now to Him who is able to do immeasurably more than all we ask or imagine, according to His power that is at work within us, to Him be glory in the church and in Christ Jesus throughout all generations, forever and ever! Amen. Ephesians 3:20,21 NIV

What do these verses tell you about God's power? How do they help you to hang onto believing He is at work even if you can't see it?

22

DESPERATE PRAYER, INCREDIBLE ANSWER

Starting full-time ministry had its humble beginnings. Revved up to change the world, the only thing standing in our way was raising a team of investors to support our work. We arranged to stay with my mom in Buffalo to begin building our financial base.

But we were shocked my mom had suffered memory loss since we last saw her and she forgot she said we could stay with her! We had no income yet, so we couldn't rent a place. Our organization wanted us to stay focused on developing our team of investors, so they didn't want us to take on employment.

We stayed with several friends over the next two weeks and tried to give our two-year-old and five-year-old a sense of stability. It was challenging to call potential partners without our own phone, and getting ready for appointments was even more complicated since we weren't sure which corner of the car trunk our shoes were.

Then to top things off, our two-year-old son stuck a screw up his nose while we were sharing about our ministry at someone's house. Off we went to the emergency room. The following day he was poking Rice Krispies into his ear. It was just a terrible time!

In the quietness of my weekly coffee shop routine, I prayed a simple but effective prayer: HELP!

I prayed specifically for...

1. a house owned by a church, so they would be patient with the rent while our income was established
2. in the South Buffalo neighborhood where we used to live
3. sidewalks
4. a large office with a phone jack and a fenced-in yard for the kids
5. $150 rent!

The following Sunday, we were driving through our old neighborhood after church. I happened to notice a cute little white split-level house with tall grass and no curtains in the windows. Hmmm...

Knocking on the neighbor's door, we learned it belonged to a church. Hmmmm... He gave us the pastor's number.

As the pastor gave us a tour, this beautiful split level was everything I had prayed for! It was in our old neighborhood, with sidewalks, an office with a phone jack, and a fenced-in yard complete with a swingset.

When we asked what the rent was, the pastor told us a very large figure and, as our faces dropped, he changed it to $175. Then he paused and looked up. "Okay, Lord," he replied to the heavens, then looked back at us and countered with, "$150 and pay whenever you are able!"

We moved in that night with our air mattress.

To reflect:
What is your reaction to this story?

To consider:
Ask and it will be given to you; seek and you will find; knock, and the door will be opened to you. For everyone who asks receives; the one who seeks finds; and to the one who knocks, the door will be opened. Matthew 7:7,8 NIV

What would you like to ask Him for today? What door would you like Him to open for you?

23

JESUS CARES ABOUT SHOWER CURTAINS

What will we eat? I asked Jesus the first morning in our new home, as I surveyed our empty kitchen. My mind was still whirling from this unbelievable housing provision. Suddenly, there was a knock on the door. Our kitchen went from empty to overflowing, as two friends from our church unloaded twelve bags of groceries they had collected. So then I asked again, W*hat will we eat?* because we had so much to choose from!

As astonishing as the Lord's provision of the actual house was, even more incredible was how He fully furnished it. He provided kitchenware, curtains, sheets, towels, beds, dressers. Everything we needed. I don't remember where it all came from, but it poured in.

One woman at church "just happened" to have an extra gas stove and her boyfriend "just happened" to be a gas stove installer. Another family "just happened" to have an extra washer and dryer sitting in their garage. A friend had an extra refrigerator not in use. A perfectly good sofa was out on the curb a few streets away.

One morning as I was getting ready to speak at a prayer

breakfast, I glanced up at the tablecloth attached with safety pins which served as our shower curtain. I said, *Y'know Lord, it would be nice to have a regular shower curtain.*

After the breakfast, a woman came up and asked somewhat apologetically, "Can you by any chance use…a shower curtain? For some reason, this one wouldn't sell at my garage sale."

This wasn't just a run-of-the-mill shower curtain. It was the premier version, with ruffled deep blue drapes which framed the shower curtain. Our Heavenly Father provides in special ways for His children!

Another time we were worried about how we would pay our $60 car insurance bill, so we prayed. The next day I was rummaging in the glove compartment of a car we had recently purchased. I was surprised to discover an old envelope hidden in a secret little space underneath the main shelf. It had a sweet note from a man to his wife which said to keep the enclosed money for an emergency. It contained $60! We couldn't trace who the couple was, so we assumed the "emergency" was ours.

We encountered challenges while we developed our investment team. My dad died, probably without knowing Jesus. Peter's mom was diagnosed as having terminal cancer. We watched my mom's memory and sense of reality continue to deteriorate.

But it also had its blessings. God faithfully provided again and again, despite our not always doing our part and being slow to trust Him. Somehow we were always able to pay our bills on time and never went without what we needed.

After two years, our group of financial investors was finally complete. In the process of building this team, we met many wonderful Christians all over the United States whom we would never have met otherwise. They not only came alongside us financially. They also believed in us, took an interest in our children, and prayed for us. The doors to their homes and food pantries were always open. They shared zoo passes, fishing poles, lake cabins and cars. My unpleasant impression of South Carolina during seminary has been replaced by sweet memories of our hospitable and generous partners there.

It is amazing that, more than 35 years later, many of our original partners are still on our team. They are so much more than ministry partners; many have become close friends. I can't begin to imagine how we could have done what we've done without them and their prayers, encouragement, and financial support.

To reflect:
Have you ever had a need met in a surprising way?

To consider:
Look at the birds of the air; they do not sow or reap or store away in barns, and yet your heavenly Father feeds them. Are you not much more valuable than they? Matthew 6:26 NIV

What does this verse say about God, and His attitude toward the smaller details of your life?

24

FLAT!

Neither one of us dared to say what we were both thinking.

After driving through isolated brush and cattle land for hours, our little family of four hadn't seen one single car. As I surveyed the Texas sun beating down on brown brambles and an endless stretch of barbed wire, I asked myself the unspoken question, *"What in the world would we do if the car had a problem?"* This was before the marvelous invention of cellphones.

We would soon find out.

Up ahead through the dust we spotted... could it be... civilization at last! The very moment our tires crossed the border of this tiny town, a jolt made it obvious we just blew a tire.

Within minutes, a tow truck appeared behind us, and a friendly gentleman jumped out to offer Peter a ride to the tire store. This town was no more than six blocks long, but they had a tire store? Before I knew it, they were back and the man was putting the new tire on for us.

"How much should we pay him?" Peter and I discussed briefly, taking inventory of our cash reserves. Turning back to thank this Good Samaritan, the man and his truck were already gone. He left as quickly as he appeared.

Buckling up again, we drove through the remaining five blocks of this little town and proceeded through hours and hours of deserted wasteland again.

How did that tire know the precise spot it should go flat? Who was that tow-truck man anyway? Did he possibly have wings?

Some might say it was a lucky coincidence. All I can say is that we have a lot of coincidences when we pray!

To reflect:
Have you ever been stranded somewhere? How did you get where you needed to be?

To consider:
God is our refuge and strength, an ever-present help in trouble. Psalm 46:1 NIV

How does it feel to know God is always present when you have trouble? Have you ever asked Him for help with your challenges?

25

S'MORES ON THE DASHBOARD

As we continued our trek west, we marveled over dinosaur footprints in Texas and slid down New Mexico's white sand dunes. Finally, one formidable frontier stood between us and our new home: Death Valley.

Flat plains of sand and empty asphalt stretched as far as the eye could see. Maybe they call it a desert because it truly is deserted. The unrelenting sun blazed so hot, that we melted s'mores on a paper towel on the front dashboard. I'm guessing we could have fried an egg on the hood if we had tried.

So there we were, speeding down the hot-as-hades highway when far on the horizon we spotted a rest stop. Just as Peter slowed down to pull in, a sudden wump-wump-wump revealed another tire problem.

We had a real mess on our hands. The hot tar pavement had melted and shredded our tire, wrapping itself around the axle. Thankfully, it happened when we were pulling into an empty parking lot. *What would we do now?* The nuts and bolts had been firmly tightened with an air gun, plus untwisting the old tire from the axle would be no easy job. Even if cellphones did exist, there would have been no coverage in this isolated place.

As we walked to the restroom, we discovered a lonely, mobile food wagon sitting in the far corner of the parking lot. You may recall this place wasn't exactly crawling with customers, and the man later told us he wasn't even sure why he had parked there. But there he was in our hour of need. For some reason, he had the equipment, muscles, and know-how needed to unwrap and remove the old tire and put on the new one! Maybe God had something to do with it?

Off we went across the hot, desolate stretch of nothingness. We reached our new home without any more car problems.

You may have guessed we started this 3,000-mile trip with noticeably used tires. We were inexperienced travelers and didn't realize the beating which tires endure when you barrel along the scenic route from Buffalo, New York, to San Bernardino, California, via Texas. You might even say we were foolish. And we were.

I am still amazed how my mistakes and human frailty don't prevent God from doing what He wants to do. In fact, they often serve as the perfect backdrop from which our compassionate Father can display His grace and power the most.

To reflect:
Have you ever gotten into a difficult situation because of an unwise choice? What do you think God's attitude toward you was at that time?

To consider:
But He led His own people like a flock of sheep, guiding them safely through the wilderness. He kept them safe so they were not afraid; but the sea covered their enemies. Psalm 78:52, 53 NLT

How does this verse change your opinion of how God sees you?

26

TIRED OF TRUSTING

We breathed a sigh of relief as we unpacked our boxes in our California home. We now had a consistent income, thanks to like-minded partners who faithfully invested in our ministry. We were about to learn that financial problems can be a lot easier to solve than other things life throws at us. But God is always there to help us catch them.

Having agreed to rent a large corner house sight unseen, we were amazed it had almost everything we had prayed for. God's answer to my prayer for sidewalks wasn't quite what I had in mind and I think reflected His sense of humor. There were sidewalks all along the front and side of the house, but they stopped at our property lines. There were no sidewalks anywhere else. I suppose I should have prayed for sidewalks that actually lead somewhere.

We were soon delighted to discover our third child, Andrew, was on the way. At my six-week checkup after his birth, the doctor noticed a lump in my throat. Several tests later, they concluded it was a growth that needed to be removed. I woke up from surgery to the news they suspected it was cancer but would know in a week.

Waiting for the biopsy results was a thought-provoking time. I thought about the shortness of life and the things we won't enjoy in Heaven: giving birth, watching children grow, sharing the Good News with others, and helping them know Jesus better.

It also was a very difficult time because I wrongly assumed mature Christians do not feel fear or anxiety. But I did, and I felt ashamed that I did. Now I realize Christians are humans with emotions, and my Father doesn't expect me to be perfect. He wanted me to rest in His arms and trust Him with my fears. The final tests revealed Hashimoto's thyroiditis, not cancer. It's harder to pronounce, but much easier to get rid of!

A few weeks later, we all came down with strep throat. While having six-month-old Andrew examined for it, I asked about a lump on the base of his spine. A specialist said it looked like spina bifida. Andrew might never walk.

I discovered it was much easier to trust God for my health than my child's.

Then all my surgery bills began to arrive—thousands and thousands of dollars. We had just drained our finances paying off bills from Andrew's birth.

At the same time, I received news that my mom's health was continuing to deteriorate and she would probably need to be put into assisted living. I was flooded with grief and condemned myself because I couldn't help.

To top it all off, my older sister, who had a thyroid surgery similar to mine, told me to expect to put on 10 to 20 pounds. I was already depressed about the 10 pounds I still had from my pregnancy with Andrew.

Instead of thinking about how God was still in control and focusing on His character, I was filled with guilt that my joy was so dependent on circumstances and I couldn't handle all this better. I dwelled on how I thought the perfect Christian should go through these things, and how far I fell short.

I was completely drained—physically, mentally, emotionally, spiritually. *Lord, I am so tired of having to trust You. I confess that my thoughts are so scattered, I just can't focus on You. But I pray You will provide, not because we are worthy but because You are merciful.*

And He did.

To reflect:
Was or is there a time you felt everything was crashing in on you? How did you cope with it?

To consider:
Be anxious for nothing, but in everything by prayer and supplication with thanksgiving let your requests be made known to God. And the peace of God, which surpasses all comprehension, will guard your hearts and your minds in Christ Jesus. Philippians 4:6,7 NASB

What encourages your heart in these verses? How could you deal with your challenges differently?

27

JESUS COMES THROUGH AGAIN

When I took Andrew back for x-rays for what they thought was spina bifida, another more experienced specialist "just happened" to walk by. After examining Andrew, the specialist concluded it was probably spina bifida *occulta*. This meant his incomplete vertebrae were at the very end of his spine, where there are no nerves attached, so they should never have any effect on him. I was so relieved!

This diagnosis was confirmed when he became a toddler, because there certainly was nothing that slowed him down. The vertebrae closed themselves up over time, and Andrew became an excellent athlete. The physician who examined his backbone during his developmental years offered him a part-time job as a teenager. This led to Andrew's current career as a physician's assistant in orthopedics. God used Andrew's undesirable condition to guide him into a well-suited career.

Back to our story from the last chapter. When the dust settled with my astronomical surgery bills, it was to our benefit that expenses from Andrew's birth were the same year as my surgery. Since our medical insurance paid 100% after we exceeded a certain amount of medical expenses, they paid most of my surgery costs. We only had to pay my surgeon $37 and a few other small bills which were very manageable.

My brother, who lived close to my mom, was able to arrange good home care for her, much better than I could have given her. She was able to stay in her own home much longer than we originally thought. I realized God loved my mom more than I did, and He would take care of her even when I couldn't.

In the process of finding the right amount of thyroid medicine for me, my dose was too high for a couple of months. This makes your heartbeat too fast and causes irritability, but it also makes you lose weight. So the extra 10 lbs. from pregnancy I was worried about just effortlessly dropped off, along with a few extra pounds!

Most of all, God wasn't surprised by the "uglies" in my life. In fact, He had allowed all these circumstances to bring my imperfections to the surface, not so I could create my own self-improvement plan, but so I could realize my absolute inability to change them.

God didn't expect me to be perfect, just yielded and trusting. He wanted to remind me that my hope does not rest on my performance, my husband, my children, good health, or my appearance. My hope is in the great, the mighty, the awesome God and His ability to transform me from the inside out. He alone is greater than any problem I have and He alone is concerned with the smallest of details.

To reflect:
On which of these things do you tend to place your hope? (husband, performance, children, health, appearance, or something else?)

To consider:
You have been chosen to know me, believe in me, and understand

that I alone am God. There is no other God— there never has been, and there never will be. I, yes I, am the Lord, and there is no other Savior. Isaiah 43:10,11 NLT

Who does this verse say is the only One we can place our hope in? What would that look like in your life?

Station Wagon Express

28

CREATIVE MESSES AND BEDTIME PRAYERS

I smiled as I spotted Julia and Daniel eating their lunches on the roof of our California home.

Homeschooling during their younger years inspired my creativity. I was determined to make homeschooling fun. The low, flat roof of our back porch safely served, on occasion, as the perfect lunchroom. Sometimes they climbed up there with their school assignments, for a change of scenery. One time I hurried outside because I thought they were jumping on the roof, only to discover the shaking was caused by our very first earthquake.

Each day was full with no wiggle room, especially when I was chasing young Andrew while I juggled homeschooling and housework. But I loved seeing their eyes light up with new truths, especially when I was the one to teach them. My heart overflowed with love for these unique beings, and I knew I was needed. Some days I wished I wasn't needed so much. At the time, it felt like this stage of life would go on forever. Now it seems like just a flicker in time.

After three years in California, our headquarters where Peter worked announced it was moving to Florida. Since houses in

Florida were less expensive and our income had increased, we were excited that we would now be able to buy our own home.

A month before Peter and I visited Florida, we made the shape of a house on graph paper and taped it to the kitchen wall. Each member of our family agreed to fill in a graph square every time they prayed for this important purchase. While Peter and I house hunted in Florida, Julia and Daniel continued praying and filling in squares in California. The last square was filled in on the exact day we looked at the house we now call home.

Over the years these walls were filled with laughter and crying and creative messes. The front door bade these young ones goodbye each morning as they headed off to school. Each month their heads grew closer to the top of the doorway. Its hardwood floors felt the transformation of tiny bare feet into energetic feet clad in soccer cleats and excited feet wobbling in prom high heels.

The walls witnessed shouts of victory from Nintendo games, closets being checked for monsters, and bedtime prayers. Its front porch watched the transformation of our family as we posed there for photos of kindergarten, high school, and college graduations. Laughter now rings through the halls again when grandkids play with their parents' old toys, which I sentimentally saved for this purpose.

I appreciate the peace of my current stage of life, although sometimes I miss the meaningful chaos of nurturing young children. Through all the changes that occurred in raising children to adulthood, Jesus' faithful provision and protection remained the same.

To reflect:
What stage of life are you currently in? Which is or was your favorite stage and why?

To consider:
There is a time for everything and a season for every activity under the heavens. Ecclesiastes 3:1 NIV

How could you enjoy your current stage of life more?

29

SHELF ON THE SHELF

Trying to find locker shelves at the store in February was about as likely as finding Easter candy in August. Unless you have a loving Heavenly Father who cares about the little things that are important to you, that is.

Starting at a new middle school, our daughter Julia was concerned about having her transition go smoothly. She was a conscientious student and liked everything well organized, which meant she really wanted shelves for her school locker. This was before online shopping, and the store clerk told me they never had any except in September.

Knowing how important this was to her, we did what we usually did: pray.

A couple of days later, I was weaving up and down the store aisles, intently searching for the usual items on my shopping list. Four-year-old Andrew was sitting in the cart.

"What's that?" he interrupted, pointing to the bottom shelf on the opposite side of the aisle. I have no idea how he could even see the bottom shelf from his vantage point in the shopping cart. Bending down to examine the mostly-empty shelf, I discovered one lonely, beat-up box with locker shelves in it! *How long had they been sitting there?* It had someone's name written on it then crossed off, like it had been set aside for a while. But the shelves inside were brand new. The price was $7.00, about half of what they usually cost.

You should have seen Julia's face light up when she saw this special answer to prayer! I'm guessing she had the most organized locker in the school.

To reflect:
What would you like God to do that would make your face light up?

To consider:
"Delight yourself in the Lord, and He will give you the desires of your heart." Psalm 37:4 NASB

Does it surprise you that the Lord loves to delight you? And that you can delight in Him? Why or why not?

30

SPELLING BEE CHAMP

"Lord, please help us study the words Daniel will be asked in the 4th-grade Spelling Bee tomorrow," we prayed together, and then dove into the list.

There were hundreds of words, and in spite of diligent daily practice, we had only reviewed a fraction of them. *How did tomorrow arrive so quickly?* I felt a pang of mom-guilt that I had not helped him more in the weeks prior.

It was almost bedtime, so we could only practice about twenty words before the big class competition. He did very well in this final hurried review, with only two words needing correction.

Joining the audience of enthusiastic parents in his classroom the next morning, I watched proudly as Daniel confidently stood his ground spelling each word correctly. Several dropped off early, and then the rest slowly were disqualified until it was just Daniel and one other student. I held my breath and prayed as the final round began. Sure and steady, Daniel breezed through the last word which his opponent missed. I felt joy and pride as I saw his huge smile as his classmates cheered and clapped loudly.

What was the final word that clinched the victory for Daniel? C-H-R-O-N-I-C.

Would you believe it was one of the few words we had covered the evening before? In fact, it was one of the two words he had misspelled during our short practice. The previous night's correction on that one little word won him the championship. Jesus had answered our prayers for Him to lead us the night before.

More than all the supportive parents combined that day, Jesus is our greatest cheerleader. He is cheering us toward the finish line. He wants us to be successful and is ready and waiting for us to ask Him to help us in whatever tasks we need to complete.

To reflect:
Do you believe God wants to help you be successful? Why or why not?

To consider:
Behold, God is my helper; The Lord is the sustainer of my soul. Psalm 54:4 NASB

What does this verse tell you about God? What would you like Him to help you with today?

31

A BIG FISH STORY

What better birthday gift could I give an avid young fisherman than a whole morning with Mom at the local fishing spot?

When Daniel was younger, he loved fishing. Peter took him whenever he could spare an hour. So this day, his 9th birthday, our mother-son outing would not be rushed. After early stops at the donut store and tackle shop, we prayed for an extra good catch to celebrate his special day.

Did I mention I was not exactly the most experienced fisherman nor the most qualified fishing guide? But I do know how to pray.

It began pretty frustratingly: worms falling off our hooks, lines getting tangled, and the only bites we got were turtles. Knowing Daniel would not get much help from a fishing rookie like me, I realized it would take an act of God to measure up to his expectations.

For me, the trip was already successful. I realized how seldom I took time just with him, and how much I loved those moments standing together before the still water and blue sky. I noticed how tall he was getting, and realized there would not be many more birthdays he would want to spend with his dear ol' mom. I had no idea I was carving a treasured memory of him poised expectantly on that dock, pole in hand.

Many prayers and two hours later…*was that a tug on his line?* His face lit up, and so did mine, as he proudly snagged a shiner. Our pail was no longer empty. The line jiggled again and he caught another…and another…and another. By the time we left for lunch, he had caught 15 fish! We shared the joy of victory together, as we drove home to proudly display the fish that *didn't* get away.

They were not very large fish, but they told a nine-year-old that Jesus still helps fishermen catch fish when they look to Him.

To reflect:
Do you think we would have enjoyed our fishing trip if we had not caught any fish? Why or why not?

To consider:
Two people are better off than one, for they can help each other succeed. If one person falls, the other can reach out and help. But someone who falls alone is in real trouble… A person standing alone can be attacked and defeated, but two can stand back-to-back and conquer. Three are even better, for a triple-braided cord is not easily broken. Ecclesiastes 4:9, 10, 12 NLT

What other gifts did God give us that day besides the fish? Is there a memory etched in your mind of a special time with someone?

32

BOUNCING PRAYERS TO HEAVEN

W*hat if the Lord doesn't answer? Do I need to help Him out a little?*
Ever since Andrew took his first steps, he lived and breathed sports. So it was little surprise when three-year-old Andrew began praying specifically for a sturdy basketball net, which was his size, for a very cheap price.

He believed God would do it more than his mother did. I worried and wondered how I would explain it to him if God didn't provide. Oh, me of little faith, you would think I would know by now.

Every time we drove past our favorite thrift store, he would exclaim, "Let's stop and see if my basketball net is there yet!" Several months and many unfruitful thrift store stops later, his faith was unshaken. He was still just as certain God was going to answer as the first time he prayed for it and often talked about "*when* I get my basketball net..."

His unwavering faith won over my doubts. I began to expect God was going to do something special.

Five months after he first prayed—the week before his 4th birthday—heaven answered. I was at the store buying the usual toilet paper and napkins when something on the clearance shelf caught my eye. I looked closer, and I couldn't believe it—a brand new child-size metal basketball rim, pole, and net was marked down from $60 to $15! I pictured God's smiling, benevolent face.

I could hardly restrain myself all week long from giving Andrew God's birthday present. It was an incredible answer to his believing, persistent prayer.

When the day arrived and Andrew unwrapped his long-awaited net, he excitedly put it together. But his attitude was also surprisingly matter-of-fact. After all, when he asked me for a grilled cheese sandwich, I gave it to him; so of course, when he asked his heavenly Father for a basketball net, he was not surprised when He gave it to him.

No wonder Jesus said we need to have the faith of a child.

To reflect:
When have you been surprised by the faith of a child?

To consider:
And he said: "Truly I tell you, unless you change and become like little children, you will never enter the kingdom of heaven." Matthew 18:3 NIV

What does this verse tell us about what God values? What would it look like for you to trust Him more like a child?

33

HAVE SUITCASE, WILL TRAVEL

"Why are we parked here?" young Andrew innocently inquired as we sat waiting in a never-ending traffic jam on the first of our two-day journey. Fortunately, no one needed a restroom (that would usually be me). After an hour or so, we were able to move again —just in time to encounter a torrential downpour.

Daniel's and Julia's suitcases tied on the roof didn't fare well and their clothes were soaked. After laying them out at the hotel to dry overnight, we had a bright idea: *Why not put the luggage in plastic garbage bags before tying them to the roof rack? This would make them more waterproof.* We would soon find out that plastic bags create a less desirable quality, too.

Off we sped the next morning, McDonald's drive-thru breakfast in hand, hoping to make up for lost time. Everything was going great until we heard a big *wump*! Pulling to the side of the freeway, we were alarmed to see what looked like Daniel's luggage back in the middle of the fast lane. Note to self: plastic bags not only make luggage waterproof, but they also make them *slippery*.

"Ha, ha, ha," Julia laughed. "Your suitcase flew off!!"

"Well, guess what," Daniel replied. "Yours is missing, too!"

Her laughter immediately stopped. *At least we knew where Daniel's was, but where was Julia's?*

Peter eventually discovered her bag in the tall weeds on the right side of the road, but how would we retrieve Daniel's? The high-speed traffic made it obvious this would be no easy task.

Before I could stop him, Peter leaped into action. Faster than a speeding bullet, he sprinted across the two lanes, snatched up the luggage with split-second accuracy, and ran back just in time to avoid having tire tracks imprinted across his shirt as the next car whizzed by. We took the luggage out of the ripped-up plastic and took extra care to secure them, and prayed for clear skies.

Would you believe our adult children mention family road trips as being among their fondest memories?

To reflect:
What is a favorite childhood memory of yours?

To consider:
Therefore I, a prisoner for serving the Lord, beg you to lead a life worthy of your calling, for you have been called by God. Always be humble and gentle. Be patient with each other, making allowance for each other's faults because of your love. Make every effort to keep yourselves united in the Spirit, binding yourselves together with peace. Ephesians 4:1-3 NLT

Which one of these qualities would be the most helpful to you in your relationships? Why?

34

OVER THE CLIFF!

Staring up at the ski slope, I felt uneasy that ten-year-old Andrew had been gone so long. It was unseasonably warm, so a layer of melted icy snow on top of the still-frozen snow made the slopes extra slippery. Prompted to pray for him, I pictured him cushioned by heavenly arms wrapped around him as I prayed for the different parts of his body.

Lord, please protect Andrew's head. Please place your protection around his arms, his legs, his backbone, his feet, his inner organs...

After what seemed like forever, I was relieved to see him finally whizzing down the slope. Joining us inside for hot chocolate, he lifted the light windbreaker he was wearing to reveal a two-inch scratch and a small bruise by his ribs.

"I just went over the side of the mountain," he calmly announced. As the day wore on, more details spilled out which convinced me something supernatural had happened.

Casually eating his lunch, Andrew explained how he had hit an ice patch, flew over the protective ramp, and tumbled twenty feet down the mountain.

"Didn't your skis hit you?"

"They flew off when I hit the rocks."

Hit the rocks? I thought with alarm. *He flew off the cliff and hit the rocks?*

"What kept you from going all the way down?"

"Oh, the trees stopped me."

You hit the trees? I gasped inside. *He flew off the side of a mountain and hit rocks and trees hard enough to make his skis fly off?*

I concluded he was probably exaggerating, until he added as an afterthought later that afternoon, "They sent the rescue squad."

The rescue squad? I cringed.

"They wanted to know where the body was. The medical staff told me they fully expected to be carrying off a dead body and were surprised to see me walking."

Andrew tumbled down the side of a mountain, hitting rocks and trees along the way without even a padded jacket to protect him, and came out with only one small scratch and a little bruise. God's hands had indeed been firmly around Andrew, and I was thankful I responded to that nudge to pray for him.

But I wasn't sorry when it rained the next day, and snow fun was canceled!

To reflect:

Have you ever sensed a nudge to pray for someone or something? How did you respond?

To consider:

Whoever dwells in the shelter of the Most High will rest in the shadow of the Almighty. I will say of the Lord, "He is my refuge and my fortress, my God, in whom I trust." Psalm 91:1,2 NIV

What picture comes to your mind when you read these verses? How does it speak to your heart? How do you think our prayers and God's protection fit together?

35

LAST CALL: ORLANDO

Exhausted. Absolutely exhausted. The delayed flight from our Colorado conference to Orlando couldn't have come at a worse time.

After ten days of meetings morning, noon, and night while shuffling children to and from childcare, I was *so* ready to be home. But Peter, our children, and I sat on the runway. One hour, two hours. Still, we waited. If you have ever tried to keep a tired but restless two-year-old sitting on your lap while confined to a narrow airplane seat, you feel my pain. There are only so many stories and games you can distract a child with while your patience grows thin and your legs grow numb.

When we bought our tickets, there were no seats available on the nonstop flights to Orlando. We had to settle for an out-of-the-way route, which added hours to the journey home. I cringed when I thought about keeping our toddler occupied while we flew from Denver all the way up to Chicago, endured a few hours layover, then flew down to Orlando from there. I poured out my distress and my longing to just go home to my ever-listening heavenly Father.

Finally, an announcement: they would pull up to the terminal so we could use food vouchers to grab something to eat. We could continue to wait, or inquire about switching flights. Anxious to move around a little, I piled our daughter into her stroller and hurried through the gate. It brought us into the middle of a very long stretch of gates with moving sidewalks, endlessly disappearing in both directions with the opening right where we got off.

Directly across from us was another gate. There, flashing right in front of my weary eyes, was what looked like a mirage. In bright letters, it shouted, "Orlando Nonstop, last call!"

The attendants must have seen the desperation on my face as I rushed over, because they welcomed me to fill the very last seat available. Adrenaline pumping, I had just enough time to tell Peter we would see him in Orlando, as they ushered me onto the plane and into a first-class seat. I had never been in first class! We buckled up and off we went, not even having to endure the usual thirty-minute wait between boarding and take-off.

I was still marveling at this wonderful turn of events when they brought me my fancy meal, complete with cloth napkins. My daughter fell asleep alongside me in my roomy seat, and I breathed a huge sigh of relief that we would soon be directly home.

In that endless stretch of gates, what were the chances our Chicago-bound flight would unload directly across from a nonstop flight to Orlando, at exactly the right time? Even three minutes later would have been too late. Is it possible that a caring Heavenly Father had opened the gates, so to speak, so His dearly-loved daughter could get some rest?

In the midst of my busyness caring for others, I sometimes forget I can crawl into my loving Father's lap, where He is delighted to allow me to just be His needy child.

To Reflect:
Do you ever get so busy taking care of others that you forget to take care of yourself?

To Consider:
Come to me, all you who are weary and burdened, and I will give you rest. Take my yoke upon you and learn from me, for I am gentle and humble in heart, and you will find rest for your souls. For my yoke is easy and my burden is light. Matthew 11:28-30 NIV

What is Jesus' attitude toward you when you are overwhelmed? What does He invite you to do?

36

STANDING - LITERALLY - ON THE PROMISES OF GOD

As our nine-year-old daughter sat despondent in a wheelchair, test results confirmed the dreaded diagnosis.

It had started during one of the most hellish whirlwinds of our lives. We were frantically preparing to move from America to East Asia before the second half of the school year began. Meanwhile, our younger daughter quickly jerked sideways while running, and injured her leg. Over the next three months, we took her to four doctors who all said the same thing: muscle sprain. But she continued to experience excruciating pain if she bent her leg or we lightly touched the top of her foot.

On December 31st, we arrived in East Asia, as planned. I watched with sadness as she hobbled on crutches up and down six flights of stairs from our apartment to the school bus. *I've had four children with numerous sprains. Given time, she'll recover... Won't she?* I tried to convince myself. But my doubts increased as her condition remained unchanged. While tending to business in a nearby country, we sought answers at an internationally acclaimed hospital.

We sought answers at an internationally acclaimed hospital

on our way to our biennial conference in another country. Several blood tests and bone scans later, the hospital staff delivered the grim verdict: reflex sympathetic dystrophy syndrome. This is a rare complication where the nerves in an injured area take on a mind of their own. It's a deceptive disease because her leg and foot looked perfectly normal, yet she experienced constant pain.

Showing us white spots on the bone scans, the doctor explained, "There is no cure. The only treatment which sometimes helps is aggressive physical therapy." She went on to caution us, "But if you push too hard, you will make it worse. The longer she has it, the less likely she will recover. And her muscles will continue to deteriorate."

Tears streamed down my face as we boarded our short flight to the conference. My previous assumptions that our daughter was just being overly dramatic and looking for attention left me overwhelmed with grief and guilt. I felt powerless to relieve the pain I saw etched on her face. But we soon found out we had unlimited power right at our fingertips.

We were invited to attend a Christian gathering in that country. Our daughter hobbled on her crutches to childcare, then Peter and I proceeded to the meeting. When we entered the auditorium and the room exploded in worship, my spirit was electrified by the unmistakable presence of God. It was unforgettable.

The speaker seemed to be talking directly to me. I desperately needed his reminder that God is a loving Father who hurts when we hurt. God felt compassion not only for our daughter's pain, but also for the anguish Peter and I felt watching her suffer. At the end of the meeting, the speaker invited anyone who needed prayer to come forward.

I was convinced that Jesus was our only hope for our daughter's recovery. So with her still in childcare, we expectantly bounded down from the upper tier to the front of the auditorium, where several of our friends joined us in asking God to heal her.

Tire Tracks

"We prayed for you this morning!" Peter announced when we arrived at childcare.

"What time?" she inquired, sitting there with her leg bent.

With her leg—which she had not been able to bend for four months—bent!

We were astonished to discover that she was healed and freed from all pain at the exact time we prayed. She was not physically with us when we prayed. Prayer knows no geographical limits! Plus, our daughter had no idea we were praying for her. This was no "power of suggestion" or psychologically-induced healing.

She was, *literally,* standing on the promises of God.

As she effortlessly climbed the winding stairs and then ran down the hall, her "of-little-faith" parents kept warning her to "take it easy." Her face was ecstatic as she jumped up and down, triumphantly waving her crutches in the air. Later she and Peter leaped into the pool, ignoring its frigid temperature. We celebrated with pizza for her and her new friends and shot spitballs at her crutches. I will never forget it.

Before returning to East Asia, we returned to the hospital to check for muscle deterioration. As we explained about our daughter's healing, the doctor was silent. After a long pause, the physician exclaimed, "The god... has been good to you!"

Yes, He had indeed been good to us! The only lingering effect of that horrible disease was for about a year her right foot flopped a little when she swam. No muscles had atrophied, though, and her foot weakness disappeared in time. She played soccer and basketball in middle school and high school with no problem.

Even the worst skeptic would have a hard time explaining what happened. A girl who had been in severe pain and unable to walk for four months "coincidentally" walked pain-free, at the exact time Christians fervently prayed for her healing. And she had no idea they were praying for her.

Perhaps the only explanation is that there is indeed an all-powerful, compassionate God who truly feels our pain, with tears glistening in His eyes and His arm wrapped around our shoulders. He doesn't promise to always perform miraculous physical healing, but the miracle of His presence and power inside of us is always within reach for those who trust in Jesus. Always.

To reflect:
Have you ever felt powerless to help yourself or someone you love? What were the details?

To consider:
In the crowd that day there was a woman who for twelve years had been afflicted with hemorrhages. She had spent every penny she had on doctors but not one had been able to help her. She slipped in from behind and touched the edge of Jesus' robe. At that very moment her hemorrhaging stopped... Jesus said, "Daughter, you took a risk trusting me, and now you're healed and whole. Live well, live blessed." Luke 8:43,44,48 MSG

What is the most meaningful part to you in these verses? Why?

37

GOD THINKS OUTSIDE THE BOX

My head and heart were reeling.

After receiving news of a loved one's sudden crisis, I quickly hopped on a flight and landed in the middle of the mess. Peter would arrive in two days. But for now, I was alone to figure out how to help many practical and emotional needs all at once. I wasn't familiar with this big city and didn't have a car, which made an already difficult task even more overwhelming.

The first "Goliath" problem towering over me was how to find enough sturdy boxes to pack up and ship this apartment's contents. I didn't want to spend more money, and how would I get to the box store and then transport big boxes? I didn't think they would fit in a taxi.

Desperately needing a break, I prayed as I walked to a department store a few blocks away. Trying on some cute clothes from the bargain rack lifted my spirits, especially since recent weight loss brought me one size smaller. Behind the privacy of that changing room curtain, between the navy blue pants and the gray capris, I cried out to the Lord, *Help! I still have no idea where to find boxes.*

At the exact moment I stepped out of the fitting room, there...right in front of me...two store clerks rolled up a large bin. Full of flattened boxes. Like they were bringing my order to me. I was stunned! *What are the chances?*

The store clerks gladly gave me all seven sturdy, large boxes. But how could I carry them back? Two angels disguised as TJ Maxx workers enthusiastically taped them all together, even making handles for easy carrying.

I couldn't control the tears rolling down my face as I commended these workers to the store manager. It was so much more than boxes, to me.

It was a reminder that I was not alone. God didn't expect me to carry these burdens all by myself. He was more than able to orchestrate the exact timing of these boxes as a gift of love and comfort to me, His dearly-loved daughter.

The next day Peter arrived and we started filling those boxes. When we discovered we needed more, I now possessed the confidence that the same Father who provided the first batch would not let us down.

Sure enough, someone in the apartment building had seen boxes scattered on some curb several blocks away. In the dark of night, Peter and I wandered through the streets searching for this lost treasure. Eventually, we struck it rich. Big boxes, little boxes, odd-sized boxes—far more than we needed.

We each grabbed as much as we could easily carry. What we had snatched ended up being the perfect shapes and sizes for odd-sized items. And it was the exact amount, as if we had calculated ahead of time how many boxes would be needed. There was only one small box and a shoebox left when the last item was packed.

The Lord doesn't promise we won't have difficulties in this life, but He promises to always, always walk alongside us in the midst of them.

To reflect:
Which part of this story can you relate to?

To consider:
"Do not fear, for I am with you; Do not anxiously look about you, for I am your God. I will strengthen you, surely I will help you, Surely I will uphold you with My righteous right hand." Isaiah 41:10 NASB

What do these verses tell you about God and His attitude toward you when you don't know what to do? How could you apply these truths?

38

NOW THAT'S CUSTOMER SERVICE

My patience wore thin after almost an hour on the phone with a customer service representative, as we waded through the "ever-so-easy" steps to return a couple of Christmas gifts. My veneer of politeness cracked when she informed me she was unable to process my request because she could not locate the information.

I informed her I had very easily pulled up the order; and in fact it was on the computer screen in front of me. My voice was matter-of-fact and objective, but a condescending attitude seeped through. I apologized. When she excused herself and put me on hold once again, I began to hear faint music in the background.

Was that a familiar Christian hymn, I wondered? As the music got louder, I distinctly heard, "I need Thee every hour, oh gracious Lord; I need Thee, oh I need Thee, Every hour I need Thee."

Immediately, I felt ashamed. I concluded this customer service rep must be a Christian—my spiritual sister—listening to Christian music to make it through the day. And here I was, making her life difficult.

The wait time allowed me to apply the song's message to the

situation. When she returned, I was in a much better mood than when she left. The music continued in the background as we wrapped up our conversation.

I was just about to comment on her excellent music choice when I realized the song was actually coming from my phone! I must have turned on my music app by mistake. I suppressed my laughter as I imagined her trying to figure out, like I was, what message I was trying to give her by playing that song.

Knowing the creative ways God can tell us what we need to hear, perhaps this well-timed message came directly from Him, reminding both of us that Jesus offers unlimited resources, no matter which side of life's challenges we are on.

Now that's what I call customer service!

To reflect:
Can you relate with this story? What did you do or say when you were in a frustrating situation?

To consider:
This High Priest of ours understands our weaknesses, for He faced all of the same testings we do, yet He did not sin. So let us come boldly to the throne of our gracious God. There we will receive His mercy, and we will find grace to help us when we need it most. Hebrews 4:15,16 NLT

What does Jesus think of you when you are weak? What temptation could you ask Him to help you with today?

39

DESPERATE CRIES

Memories of her frantic cries invaded my groggy half-consciousness the next morning. Throughout the day my memory was haunted by her pleading eyes piercing through the screen door, like someone hanging onto the edge of a cliff by her fingernails.

What really gnawed at my heart was how she instinctively realized her own resources were completely exhausted, and I had the power to save her. She knew that without help, her death within a few days was imminent. Over and over again I was stirred with great compassion as I recalled her huge festering wound and desperate pleas.

And I am not even a cat lover (and my apologies to those who are).

When we first arrived at the retreat center, she appeared out of the wilderness. Our younger daughter was deeply moved and fed her bread and milk. As I feared, this mangy feline became a permanent fixture at our doorstep. But seeing my daughter's compassion melted my apathy and soon I, too, was hooked.

When we left two days later, we told the retreat manager about the cat and prayed God would take care of her. In the following days I couldn't get her off my mind, wondering what had become of her.

Imagine our relief when a family adopted her! She was pregnant, but because she was on the verge of starvation, the babies had died, causing a severe infection that would have taken her life within a few days. The family's young sons set up a lemonade stand and earned the money needed for medical care. As she recovered, she ate and ate. After such tender loving attention, we hardly recognized it was the same cat when we saw her photo. It was the kind of happy ending you hope for.

There were several things I learned about the heart of God through this experience. *What kind of God is this,* I wondered, *who bends down from His almighty throne and gently places a "worthless" cat in a loving family? If He took care of this unwanted-and-left-to-die creature, surely He is interested in caring for us for whom He gave His Son's life.*

The cat looked disgusting, and I was repulsed by her friendly efforts to rub against me. Unlike my reaction, God welcomes us with open arms no matter how dirty and smelly our lives are. He even allowed our festering disease—sin—to rub off as His own. I can have complete confidence that He will not reject me or any ugly struggles I bring before Him.

But what struck me the most was the strong wave of compassion her helpless cries aroused in me. If a non-cat lover such as myself is moved so deeply, how passionately my Heavenly Father must respond when I, His child, cry out to Him. He may not answer the way I had hoped, but it is a great comfort to realize His heart always goes out to me.

Always.

Lastly, I was reminded of the power of the prayer of powerlessness. When I remember that pitiful cat's expectant look, it reminds me to lay aside my self-sufficiency and come to God empty-handed. I am really good at mustering up my own efforts and forgetting to invite God into my situation. When I admit my desperate need for Christ instead of trying to control the outcome myself, the compassion and power of the universe show up.

How amazing the Lord used a desperate, worm-infested, half-dead creature to teach me so many valuable lessons.

Maybe I am a cat lover after all.

To reflect:
Which character in this story can you most identify with? Why?

To consider:
For His unfailing love toward those who fear Him is as great as the height of the heavens above the earth. He has removed our sins as far from us as the east is from the west. The Lord is like a father to His children, tender and compassionate to those who fear him. Psalm 103:11-13 NLT

Does anything in these verses surprise you? Which part is the most meaningful to you?

40

GOD'S FACE IN THE WIND

A loud crash on our family room roof alerted us that a dangerous Category 4 hurricane was about to barrel down our street. Peter quickly tried to determine if the big branch that fell had damaged the house while I bolted to prepare our safest bedroom for our family to ride out the storm.

Listening to the wind lash mercilessly against the window as I set up mattresses and blankets, I was awestruck by this unbridled power that uprooted massive trees at a whim. Suddenly, it was as if I heard a quiet but authoritative voice above the howling:

"I am much more powerful than this wind!" the Lord seemed to say.

It felt like everything stood still. This was a sacred moment, when God unexpectedly chose to reveal Himself to me. Looking up toward the heavens, I worshipped Him for His inconceivable greatness. Then before I could get back to my work, I heard something else in my heart that both surprised and disturbed me:

"And that power lives in you!"

It stopped me in my tracks. Looking outside at the unmistakable evidence of an invisible force at work, I felt humbled that I had not seen any hurricane-force Presence of the Lord in my life for quite some time. I thought about the spiritual meaning. *What is it that keeps wind from blowing through? Closed doors. Then what is keeping His stronger-than-this- storm Spirit from showing His evidence through me? Closed doors in my soul.*

So I stood there during that holy, storm-driven epiphany and invited Jesus into any areas of my life that I had not yet consciously given Him permission to enter.

While we snuggled together in the safe room that night, Charley rearranged our neighborhood and continued north. The next morning my son and I drove through what now looked like a war zone. We gawked at the huge trees strewn across roads, their immense roots tearing holes in lawns and shattering sidewalks. We couldn't help but laugh at the small planes at the private airport, twisted upside down right next to a flight school advertisement posted on the chain-link fence that said "Learn to Fly."

I experienced spiritual revival in the months that followed. It wasn't hurricane winds; it was like a gentle breeze that accompanies a soft summer rain. He revealed my "shut doors" of self-sufficiency, and ways I still tried to control my circumstances and other people instead of trusting Him.

His Word became very meaningful again. There was fresh spiritual energy springing up in me, and renewed enthusiasm about my faith.

Wind itself cannot be seen. It's the impact the invisible wind has on visible objects that tells us there's wind and how strong it is. Similarly, God chooses to show the reality of His Spirit by "blowing" His wind through our lives so others can see He exists and how powerful He is. Jesus refers to the Holy Spirit as being like the wind, in John 3:8.

I told the Lord I want to be a hurricane for Him, not a wimpy breeze. I asked Him to make His presence unmistakably seen in my life so He has an impact on everyone I encounter. I desired

Tire Tracks

His Spirit's wind to blow through me, strong and abundantly fruitful for Him. Unlike a hurricane whose path brings destruction, I want to be a holy storm who leaves behind a trail of His life-giving presence.

God's love for us is wildly powerful and not always predictable—like a hurricane. As Aslan is described in Chronicles of Narnia, "He isn't safe…but He's good."

To reflect:
When have you experienced the greatest display of power in nature? What could you conclude about God's power, from what you witnessed?

To consider:
I pray that God, the source of hope, will fill you completely with joy and peace because you trust in Him. Then you will overflow with confident hope through the power of the Holy Spirit.
Romans 15:13 NLT

Are you experiencing this kind of power in your life? If not, but you would like to, what do you need to do?

From Wheels to Wings

41

STOP THAT PLANE

A flat tire on the desolate highway at 4:00 am, on the way to an international flight.

A twelve-year-old who has stepped into a swarm of fire ants.

A 3-year-old who badly needs a bathroom.

A dead battery.

A dying cellphone.

What do they all have in common? They were part of the lesson God was about to take me through called "I am Not in Control but God Is."

Our son Andrew and I had been invited to join my friend Jan and her son for a conference she was speaking at in South Africa. Going to Africa had always been her dream, so she planned once-in-a-lifetime adventures before and after the conference.

But there we were, rushing from Orlando to meet Jan and Steven at the Tampa airport, when a tire blew. We had not had a flat tire for 15 years. Now that every minute counted, we were stranded.

No road signs were in sight to tell the emergency road

service our location, so their receptionist informed me that they couldn't help. As we waited and prayed for someone to pass by, Andrew stepped into a pile of fire ants and our four-year-old announced she needed a bathroom.

Jan called me every few minutes for updates. We heaved a big sigh of relief when a semi-truck finally stopped and helped Peter change the tire. Jumping into our van, Peter turned the key. Nothing. We had left the door open while waiting, so the battery was now dead. The trucker could not back up to jumpstart us, so our only option was to wait for someone else from his company to come and give us the needed boost.

The minutes ticked away.

By now my cell phone battery was almost dead, and Jan sounded more and more like I was feeling: panicked! "The flight is leaving in 15 minutes! You *have* to be here!"

Still desperately praying for Jesus to get us there on time, our battery jumpstart arrived and we shot off, my stomach doing somersaults. The suspense built as we peaked the bridge right before the airport entrance. *Would we make it?*

The second we pulled up, Jan's husband grabbed our luggage and somehow sped us past customs and directly onto the plane, seconds before they shut the door. Whew! One minute longer, and we would have been waving to the plane as it flew over the airport parking lot. There were so many details I was not in control of, yet God got us there.

After reaching a cruising altitude over the Atlantic Ocean, I excitedly explored the double-decker plane. I wandered up and down the stairs and carefully examined the overnight flight packets. Adrenaline pumping, I didn't get any sleep on that 25-hour flight.

We landed in what seemed like another world.

To reflect:
Can you think of a time when you felt out of control?

To consider:
"For I know the plans I have for you," declares the Lord, "plans to prosper you and not to harm you, plans to give you hope and a future." Jeremiah 29:11 NIV

How could you relax more in situations out of your control if you knew He has a good plan for you in the midst of what feels like chaos?

42

LOOK OUT!

"Quick! Get away from the table!" The guard frantically gestured to us, pointing up at the roof of the takeout stand we were sitting next to.

We gasped as we glanced up. A huge baboon was about to leap onto the picnic table to steal our sandwiches. But I was more intrigued than afraid, my mind whirling with all the amazing sights and sounds of South Africa. I was still savoring the surprise of ostriches nonchalantly wandering along the road; hundreds of penguins surfing and diving at the beach; and the unique beauty of Cape Point and Table Mountain. And now, we were about to lose our lunches to a creeping primate!

After eating our food a safe distance from the roof, we headed for the restroom. I jumped back as one of these hairy creatures sauntered out of the entrance. We definitely were not in America. Meanwhile, the uniformed guard was stalking through the parking lot, club poised to keep the baboons at bay. Judging by the number of these bold beasts relaxing on car roofs, I found it oddly delightful that the guards were losing the battle.

Jan feared her son might be bored on this Africa trip, so she invited my twelve-year-old son Andrew and me to join them. But the Lord had so much more of an agenda in mind than giving her son a playmate.

All these fascinating sights and sounds awakened an adventurer's heart I had no idea was there. I regretted that I had waited until my forties before traveling overseas.

A big reason I had not traveled internationally sooner is that as a child, my home was not always a safe place. I had subconsciously vowed to go only where circumstances were predictable, and I could plan ahead and be in complete control. Overseas presented too many unknowns.

It was a big step of faith to go to South Africa. But this trip helped me realize it is an illusion to think I am ever in control of my safety. The Lord knew He needed to gently lead me out of my self-protective bubble and teach me to depend on His protection. This was a necessity for the adventures He had in mind for my future.

Somewhere along the line, I realized life's most amazing experiences lie just outside my comfort zone. Stepping outside my familiar world requires depending on God instead of myself, drawing me closer to Him.

To reflect:
When was the last time you did something outside of your comfort zone?

To consider:
And without faith it is impossible to please God, because anyone who comes to Him must believe that He exists and that He rewards those who earnestly seek Him. Hebrews 11:6 NIV

How could having faith in God give you the courage to do new things? What would you step out and do, if you knew you would be safe and successful?

43

STORM OF ALL STORMS!

D*on't look down!* I repeatedly told myself, glancing away from the ravine as we wound our way up. We finally arrived at a beautiful hot springs resort at the top of this tortuous mountain road, where the conference was about to begin.

The other-worldliness surrounding me at the top of the mountain made me forget my fears on our way up. Full of wonder, I explored the meandering pathway lined with tiny round thatched-roof houses, while natural hot spring pools scattered here and there shot up wisps of steam, swirling and dissolving into the brisk air.

Soon hundreds of exuberant believers from all over the world began to arrive. When our combined voices belted out the song, "We Want to See Jesus Lifted High," the whole room shook with the presence of God.

A gigantic food tent, similar in size to half a football field, joyfully served a mystery mush of potatoes and unidentified meat at most meals. Even eating became an act of faith after I observed the hundreds of dirty dishes being dipped into the same small bin of soapy water. Without rinsing them, they were dried off with a well-used towel and stacked for the next meal.

God safely carried me up these mountain roads so I could experience something extraordinary. Unforgettable. My world was enlarged, and I would never be the same again. *But could I trust Him to carry me back down the mountain?*

The last two days of the conference, Jan and Steven had business down in Capetown. This left 12-year-old Andrew and me without Jan to guide us through the unknowns of international travel. A few hours after their taxi faded into the distance, the wind began to pick up.

That evening, ninety mph wind gusts roared inland, uprooting trees, flattening homes, and then barreling across our mountain resort. My panic increased as the winds grew fiercer, shaking the frail house we were staying in and slamming heavy rain against our windows. We later learned it was the worst storm South Africa had experienced in 50 years. But while it was happening, I had no idea what was going on.

Many questions swirled in my brain. *What's going on? What should I do? How long do South African storms like this last? Will Jan make it back or will Andrew and I be stranded here?* My questions were left unanswered because everyone had disappeared to brace themselves for the storm.

We were scheduled to leave two days later, but the winds were so strong they were blowing the nearby waterfalls sideways. All I could think of was, *How in the world are we going to get back down this mountain?* I imagined our journey brought to an abrupt end as our car blew off the side of the cliff.

Terrified, I tried to call Jan on a payphone. Unfortunately, I had no idea how to connect to an international number. Then I somehow reached Peter in Florida to ask him to pray. He was understandably concerned and exclaimed, "I will do anything and pay anything, whatever it takes to get you home safely!" I felt very cared for, but a big ocean stretched between us. Any help Peter might be able to offer would be a long time in coming.

The only person I had no trouble getting through to who could actually do something was...God.

I spent most of the night huddled in the half-darkness of our small kitchen, as the winds smashed mercilessly against the fragile house. A large tree branch menacingly rap-rap-rapped on the roof while Andrew somehow slept. He had an appetite for adventure, so I have no idea how he slept through this one. Jet lag and a simple trust in God, most likely.

Bent over my Bible in desperate prayer, I rummaged through Psalms and found assurance of His protection. I poured out my helplessness and fears to Him. Moment by anxious moment He watched over us all night long.

When the first rays of morning broke through, we surveyed the aftermath of the storm's fury. It had taken out its frustration on the enormous food tent, which was twisted into a crumpled heap. A large piece of the main building's roof had been blown off, and the electricity was out.

Conference members trickled into the darkened meeting room to sing and pray. As we joined hands and claimed God's victory over the power of darkness, suddenly the room was flooded with light as the electricity popped back on! Much to my relief, Jan and Steven made it back to the conference with no problem. I braced myself for the frightening trip back down the winding road the next day.

But that scary mountain ride never happened! No one had mentioned the tunnel that cut a straight downward path through the middle of the mountain. The driver who took us up the winding road apparently avoided the tunnel because he didn't want to pay the tolls. So we blissfully descended without even a glimpse of the precipice I feared.

So many of the things we worry about never happen. My Heavenly Father knew all along there was a tunnel, and fully intended to take care of me. I would be much better off if I thought more about His character and promises and less about my fears.

To Reflect:
What are you afraid of?

To Consider:
"Do not fear, for I am with you; Do not anxiously look about you, for I am your God. I will strengthen you, surely I will help you, Surely I will uphold you with my righteous right hand."
Isaiah 41:10 NASB

How could the truths in this Bible verse help you when you feel afraid?

44

AFRICAN SAFARI, ANYONE?

We silently climbed into the back of the jeep at 5:00 am and then the driver accelerated into the wilderness through total darkness. When the tour guide suddenly switched on his searchlight to reveal an unsuspecting elephant or wildebeest, I forgot all about the warm bed I had left behind. It was thrilling to see these creatures roaming in their natural habitat.

Our two 12-year-old boys had already sampled zebra burgers and wildebeest. Our grand finale was four days of discovering these animals alive and kicking. Several safari sightings later, I took another big step outside my comfort zone. I swallowed my fear of heights and signed up to soar above the wild kingdom in a hot air balloon. *Am I crazy?* I wondered. But I began to realize there were experiences in life I didn't want to miss that required extra courage.

It was surreal watching the giant balloon slowly come to life. I can still hear the rush of the fiery torch blasting hot air into a disheveled pile of fabric flattened in the dirt as it was transformed into a majestic multicolored bubble. Clamoring into the basket before it rose too high was thrilling. I hung onto the side of the basket tightly as we floated upward.

It was breathtaking to glimpse the first splinters of orange spreading across the horizon. As we rose, so did the sun. It lit up the grasslands below where we caught a birds-eye view of zebras running wild and free and a myriad of birds and African bushes. Then, it was over all too soon. My cup of adventure was full, yet starving for more.

We said goodbye to the resident hippopotamus in the safari resort waterhole and were soon flying the friendly skies back to America. Staring out the plane window at the clouds, I recalled the extraordinary experiences of those ten days. I especially contemplated a significant promise I made to God during that time. Realizing that as a little girl I had vowed to control my own safety, I made a new promise. *Lord, I will never again allow reasonable risks to keep me from following Your will.*

I would have missed so much if I had stayed in my familiar world and refused to step out of my comfort zone. Besides, thinking I am ever actually in charge of my safety is an illusion.

Only God has complete authority over everything and is always watching over me.

To reflect:
Can you think of a time you stepped outside your comfort zone? Were you glad or did you regret it?

To consider:
Have I not commanded you? Be strong and courageous. Do not be afraid; do not be discouraged, for the Lord your God will be with you wherever you go. Joshua 1:9 NIV

What difference would this verse make in your life when considering doing something new or scary?

45

FROZEN IN HISTORY

I watched in horror and unbelief as the plane smashed into the World Trade Center. With a jolting explosion, the towering skyscraper collapsed in billowing smoke and fire.

Still in a jet lag stupor after returning from Africa the night before, this horrific television newscast seemed unreal. I felt sick with grief as the extent of destruction from this attack unfolded.

But even in the midst of the tragic loss of thousands of lives, some individuals were spared through strange quirks of circumstances. For example, one cashier who usually worked mornings in the World Trade Center wasn't scheduled until the afternoon that day. He had a co-worker who was late to work that morning because her car was stolen the night before. She was filing a report at the police station when the planes hit.

We also experienced God's watchful care over us personally during this time. Jan originally reserved our return flights for September 11, but she rescheduled when she discovered September 9 was much cheaper. As the television newscaster announced that all flights were canceled immediately, the consequences of what could have happened to us sunk in. Planes already in the air heading to or from the United States had to land at the closest country and stay there until given permission to continue home.

If Jan had not changed the dates, we would have been stranded on some other continent for at least two weeks. Of course, this is nothing compared to those who lost their lives, but it did matter. Peter had already been graciously watching our four-year-old for 12 days, and I had a bad sinus infection that needed medical attention.

I don't know why our flights were changed so we were safe, but the flights of those who perished on those ill-fated flights were not. I don't know why I was comfortable at home while thousands in New York City were running for their lives. God used this sobering experience to remind me I don't have to know everything, and I don't have to be in charge. He has the future covered and will direct the details.

To reflect:
What troubling question would you like to ask God?

To consider:
"For my thoughts are not your thoughts, neither are your ways my ways," declares the Lord. "As the heavens are higher than the earth, so are my ways higher than your ways and my thoughts than your thoughts." Isaiah 55:8,9 NASB

How can the truths about God in these verses give you peace about situations you don't understand?

46

BROKEN HEART FOR THE CITY

So...many...people. Yet Jesus loved each one as if they were the only person in the world.

One month after the September 11 terrorist attack on the World Trade Center, I found myself staring in deafening silence at ragged remnants of bent steel. They jutted out from a pile of rubble where the Twin Towers once stood, foul-smelling smoke still billowing upward. It's one thing to see this on television, and quite another to stand in front of it. What started as a mercy mission to offer comfort and hope to the survivors ended up profoundly impacting my life.

It didn't sink in that this was more than a demolition site until we approached Battery Park. Long rows of teddy bears and flowers representing the victims stretched out in front of us. It was a powerful visual reminder that each person killed left a gaping hole in the hearts of so many loved ones.

Tears streamed down my face as the magnitude of gut-wrenching loss began to register. It was so difficult to gaze at photos of once-happy families. These were intermixed with countless letters such as "Dear Daddy, I hope you are happy even though you are dead. We are going to celebrate your birthday," or "Missing: beloved son, notify us immediately if seen."

Fire and police stations around the city also displayed the faces of those who heroically died trying to rescue those trapped inside the buildings. Everywhere we turned we encountered the walking dead: those alive but still in shock, having lost life as they once knew it.

I've heard it said, "There are no atheists in fox holes." Similarly, there were no religious restrictions in a city where their illusion of being in control of their destiny had collapsed. The church we attended needed its fourth overflow room, and people were still lined up out the door to get in.

Our team of six gave out 1,000 inspirational magazines in three days. We offered them to first responders, store clerks, and the National Guard. We shared them around the subway, down the streets, in front of the memorial flowers, on elevators… everywhere our feet touched. The airport manager, who knew four of the flight attendants who died and witnessed their plane crash into the Twin Towers, gladly gave us complete freedom to distribute magazines in the airport.

Most people gratefully took these messages of God's comfort and hope, like thirsty sojourners given a drink of water. Many said thanks, and several came back for extras to pass on to friends.

I was thrilled the local government allowed me to draw sidewalk art on busy Broadway, right outside city hall and less than half a mile from Ground Zero. My drawing of Jesus weeping with outstretched arms was a great conversation starter as passers-by stopped to look. I was able to share that Jesus felt their grief and some gladly allowed us to pray for them.

How do you forget people like the waitress who hung onto every word, then gratefully accepted our prayers and an extra copy of the magazine for her son? He was a construction worker who was traumatized by the initial clearing of debris and bodies.

Tire Tracks

The distribution center accidentally gave us a stack of Korean magazines, along with the English ones. We kept one copy as we handed the rest back, in case God had given us the Korean ones for a reason. Sure enough, our taxi driver to the airport as we returned home was Korean. He was deeply moved that the magazine was in his own language.

When my friends and I boarded our flight, I left part of my heart behind. It was strange for this small town girl to feel so at home in a big city. I loved the energy of big city life and how easy it was to connect with so many people. Talking about Jesus with people whose hearts were searching felt like what I was created for.

God was preparing me for something ahead.

To reflect:
Can you think of a time someone offered you comfort and hope when you needed it?

To consider:
Praise be to the God and Father of our Lord Jesus Christ, the Father of compassion and the God of all comfort, who comforts us in all our troubles, so that we can comfort those in any trouble with the comfort we ourselves receive from God. 2 Corinthians 1:3, 4

How does this verse describe God? Knowing this about Him, what could you ask Him to give you comfort in today? Who could you offer comfort to?

47

MY SURPRISING BIRTHDAY GIFT

I couldn't believe the song playing on my friend's car stereo! It brought back visions of a conference a few months earlier in the mountains of South Africa. Hundreds of energetic hand-clapping, foot-stomping believers passionately sang,"We want to see Jesus lifted high, a banner that flies across this land, that all men may see the truth and know, He is the way to Heaven."

I loved that song, plus it held so many special memories! I had assumed it was unique to the conference but here it was, on a double CD set of worship songs. I couldn't justify paying $25 just to enjoy that one song. It was almost my birthday, so I sent up a quick prayer, *Lord, could you please give me that song for my birthday?*

Then I forgot about my request.

A week or two later, I absentmindedly browsed through a thrift store while I waited for my daughter to finish dance class. On top of the endless rows of clothes racks were thousands of small clear plastic bags. These jumbled messes were filled with everything you can think of: Christmas cards, kitchen utensils, jewelry, last year's graduation napkins.

I never look up at those bags. But for some odd reason, as I was flipping through the short-sleeved shirts, I paused and glanced up. Right in front of me, of the myriads of bags I could be looking at, was a bag of six worship song tapes. One of the songs listed on the cassette facing me leaped out. It was, "We Want to See Jesus Lifted High." This bagful of beautiful praise and worship music was 95¢. Not even a dollar!

What are the chances out of thousands of bags of miscellaneous junk, the exact song would be in the exact location I just happened to look up at, even with that song facing out for me to see? For 95¢?

What kind of a God delights in answering the fleeting birthday request of His daughter by somehow orchestrating the domino effect of this perfect sequence of events? The kind whose ways are far beyond our understanding (Isaiah 40:28).

The kind of God who smiles at us with delight and loves us far beyond measure. The kind of God who longs to give to us far more than we want Him to give. The kind of God who loves to hear about our deepest longings and our slightest whims and, when He chooses to, can easily arrange special surprises. Like my birthday gift.

The kind of God we can trust with everything!

To reflect:
How would you define prayer? What kind of things do you usually pray for?

To consider:
For this reason the Lord is ready to show you mercy; He sits on his throne, ready to have compassion on you. Indeed, the Lord is a just God; all who wait for Him in faith will be blessed. Isaiah 30:18 NET

What is God's attitude toward you? What deep longing could you trust Him with today?

48

AN UNMISTAKABLE ANSWER

Loud, forceful shouting jolted Peter out of his jetlag fog. It sounded like two men fighting.

In a prayer meeting?

Alarmed, Peter opened his eyes and discovered two Asian men intensely praying together. Of all things, they were praying! This encounter at an overseas conference started a series of events which led to a new, unexpected chapter in our lives.

Peter's job at the time required occasional trips overseas to meet with those for whom he served. Peter is a faithful, consistent man who prefers his familiar routine. But much like me with my Africa trip, God had been gently pushing Peter out of his comfort zone. He had been feeling a strange restlessness, like God had something else for us to do.

So while soaring over the Pacific Ocean to this conference, Peter earnestly sought the Lord's guidance. As he searched through the Bible, a verse jumped out that talked about being a "doorkeeper." Another verse talked about living among the people whom you are serving. It made him wonder about filling a support role overseas instead of at the U.S. headquarters.

Lord, I am even willing to just be a doorkeeper for you, Peter responded.

The bumpy narrow-miss rides on door-less vehicles didn't phase him as much this time, but he was astonished by the hotel where the events were taking place. It was an intimidating maze of buildings, literally the size of a city. These meetings included people from around the world.

After witnessing at the prayer meeting what fervent crying out to God sounds like, Peter realized he had never prayed that way for anything. So early the next morning he passionately shouted in his soul for God to show him His will for our future—not out loud, being the considerate type who didn't want to alarm his roommate. At a breakfast meeting thirty minutes later, the Lord began to respond to the call of Peter's heart.

Carl, an accountant in a big Asian city, explained, "We're going on a furlough for six months, so there won't be anyone in our city to do the finances." Then he half-joked, "Unless you want to come fill in for us."

But for Peter, it was no joke. Silently he wondered, *Is this God's answer to my prayers? Would Nancy agree to go? What would my supervisor say?*

Peter is not one to follow circumstances as signs from God unless they are backed up by God's Word, prayer, and wise counsel. The encounters that followed seemed nothing less than supernatural.

First of all, he kept bumping into Carl. Everywhere. There were many guests spread out in this huge labyrinth of structures, and Carl appeared at every turn! They both began to wonder what was going on.

As Peter tried to concentrate on the messages, a song he hadn't heard in years suddenly flooded his mind, "Come and join the reapers, all the kingdom seekers…" (*Faithful Men* by Twila Paris.) He returned to his room to read his Bible. Romans 10:13-15 (NIV) jumped out:

"Everyone who calls on the name of the Lord will be saved. How, then, can they call on the One they have not believed in? And how can they believe in the One of whom they have not heard? And how can they hear without someone preaching to them? And how can anyone preach unless they are sent? As it is written: 'How beautiful are the feet of those who bring good news!'"

Many other verses he turned to declared the same message: *Go overseas to help others know God.*

Wondering if this was indeed the Lord guiding him, he asked his roommate's opinion. His friend responded, "With your skills and experience, it would be a privilege even to be a *doorkeeper*."

Have you ever heard anyone use that unusual word, "doorkeeper?" On the flight there, it was the exact word Peter read in the Bible and used in his prayer of surrender.

After Peter returned home, we sat on a bench overlooking the fountain in downtown Orlando. He puzzled over what these things meant and asked me, "Nancy, would you be willing to go?"

"Why wouldn't I?" I responded. God had already prepared me through my South Africa and New York City trips. I felt the same kind of restlessness Peter did, and I concluded I could tolerate anything for three months. Our two youngest children were in 9th grade and kindergarten, so we could homeschool for a few months and return in time for Andrew's high school basketball season.

Peter reluctantly approached his supervisor, Bill. Their department consisted of three people who juggled the responsibilities of six, so Peter didn't expect him to be very enthused about the idea. But Bill immediately responded, "That would be a wonderful experience for you. By all means, go!"

We packed our bags and jumped into God's unforgettable adventure.

During our three months in East Asia, we fell in love with

these kind-hearted people. When our feet landed again on American soil, we knew we had to go back. Three years later, we returned to East Asia for one year. One year stretched into ten years. It was an unspeakable privilege to help people there.

What were those two Asian men praying so passionately for? We never found out. But my guess is, they prayed for the Lord to send more of His messengers to Asia.

I know two who responded.

To reflect:
How do you find wisdom and make decisions?

To consider:
You will show me the way of life, granting me the joy of Your presence and the pleasures of living with You forever. Psalm 16:11 NLT

Can you share about a time you asked God to guide you, or you read the Bible for wisdom? According to this Bible verse, where would trusting His guidance lead you?

49

THE WONDER OF BAGELS

"*Look!* They have bagels!" I exclaimed our first morning back in the United States.

"And cereal—see, cereal!" our younger daughter excitedly responded, as we investigated the hotel's breakfast buffet. A couple sitting nearby stared at us like we were rather strange. But when you return to the U.S. after living in a developing country, the world is full of amazing discoveries. There are so many delights those who haven't lived overseas take for granted, because they were never without them.

I didn't realize how much of a "third-culture kid" our daughter had become until I saw the wonder in her eyes over everyday conveniences. She was delighted with the drinking fountain at the airport. You would never want to drink from a water fountain in our Asian city because tap water must be boiled. So the idea of pressing a button and having water you can immediately drink was remarkable. She also marveled over the dishwasher. I could almost see her calculating how much time it would save her standing in front of the sink.

After two years in East Asia, we spent the summer in the

U.S.A. I stared upward in our apartment kitchen, not able to see the top of the huge refrigerator. Ours in Asia was half the size. And the oven! I couldn't get over how big it was. I was grateful we had a small portable one in Asia, but this American contraption fit three pans at the same time. Three! And all the appliances here were so simple to run—I was astounded that I could turn them on so easily. I couldn't read any of the dials on my pint-sized washer in Asia, so I only used the one setting I knew.

And the sky—oh, how deep the blue, how white the clouds. My heart burst out in worship at the overwhelming beauty I rarely noticed before we moved. It was truly remarkable, after living with gray polluted skies most of the time overseas. How wonderful it was to pedal a bicycle on bike lanes that have only bikes, passing trees and flowers without the stress of dodging endless vehicles of every shape and size.

Being able to ask for directions and understand the answer. Stores where I could read all the signs and see familiar foods on the shelves. Tortilla chips. Low-fat yogurt. Ready-made salads. Being able to eat grapes and berries raw. Wow! Grocery shopping was like Christmas.

We loved our time overseas. It was worth any inconvenience required. One bonus was the "gratitude glasses" we received, which made it possible to see some of the big and little blessings God has given us in America. Each visit back home renewed our gratefulness for the kind Father who showers us with simple pleasures.

Have you thanked God for bagels today?

To reflect:
What would you miss if you suddenly were without it?

To consider:
The Lord is merciful and compassionate, slow to get angry and

filled with unfailing love. The Lord is good to everyone. He showers compassion on all his creation. All of Your works will thank You, Lord, and Your faithful followers will praise You.
Psalm 145:8-10 NLT

What would you like to thank God for today?

50

CHARGING THE DARKNESS

Our ten years overseas were scary, fun, and life-changing — sometimes all at the same time. Charging forward with the many exciting opportunities, we didn't notice how living overseas for ten years had affected us, each in different ways.

We moved back to America to work with international students in New York City. But shortly after our arrival, we were forced to face the reality of our fragile emotional health. It became apparent Peter was suffering from something similar to Post Traumatic Stress Disorder (PTSD).

When our organization's member care discovered what was happening, we were assigned to extended recovery in Florida instead of ministry in New York City. It's the only time I can remember angrily challenging God about the wisdom of His choices in my life. I kicked and screamed on the inside worse than any two-year-old. The magic of living in Florida had worn off.

Orlando was a great place to raise our four children during the 18 years before moving overseas. But as they grew older, I longed for a God-sized challenge that would make more use of my experience and giftings. I felt like I was sitting on the back burner, waiting for something to happen.

East Asia was my "sweet spot." I loved big city life. It thrilled me that our apartment was the center of so many lively parties and life-changing conversations. We built many treasured friendships, which continue to be a meaningful part of our lives. I already envisioned a similar ministry in New York City, and the "back burner" of Orlando was the last place I wanted to live.

After traveling the world, how could I return to things as they were before? How could I have any kind of significant spiritual impact in Orlando? I incorrectly concluded that I had loved my work overseas more than I loved God, so He stuck me on the back shelf of a dark closet. I would never be used in significant ways again.

Nothing could be further from the truth. I am ashamed of how I doubted Jesus. I have thanked Him many times for patiently listening but not giving in to my immature tantrums and not giving me what I thought I wanted. Now I can wholeheartedly say there's nowhere else I would rather live.

Placing us back in Orlando was the kindest and wisest thing He could do. It provided exactly what each family member needed, even though I could not see it at the time. After a period of much-needed rest, I now have an online ministry that reaches all around the world. Life here is definitely not the dark closet I had imagined.

Outward circumstances were only part of the problem. Often, the most formidable challenges that require the greatest courage and faith are the battles inside of us, not around us. Our first two years back in America were by far the most difficult time in Peter's and my lives, and put quite a strain on our marriage.

I had been confident in how to juggle life overseas, and I knew what to do to help someone replace spiritual darkness with Jesus' light. But I lacked the slightest clue about how to walk through Peter's PTSD darkness. Plus, wading through my own adjustments left me emotionally exhausted, with little energy remaining to come alongside him.

Any illusion of being in control crumbled, and the only things left to cling to were Jesus and the promises in the Bible. I chose to continue to cling to Him and His Word. And so did Peter.

I still pause in grateful amazement as I remember how Jesus was our solid rock through that Category 5 hurricane of life. He restored joy in our marriage, even though Peter still deals with lingering limitations. By God's grace, we now enjoy closer companionship and deeper love than we ever have. I cannot imagine life without Peter.

To reflect:
Have you ever been angry with God? What do you think God would do if you told Him exactly how you feel?

To consider:
"For I know the plans I have for you," says the Lord. "They are plans for good and not for disaster, to give you a future and a hope. In those days when you pray, I will listen. If you look for me wholeheartedly, you will find me. I will be found by you," says the Lord... Jeremiah 29:11 NLT

How would your life be different if you believed what the Bible says about God and your situation more than you believed your view of your circumstances?

Final Destination

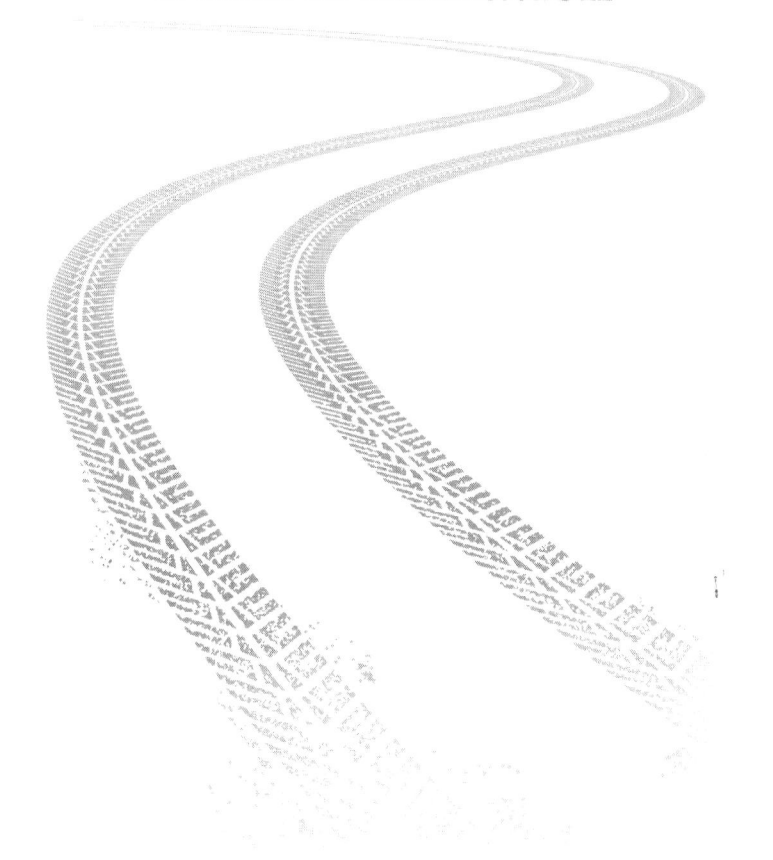

51

LOST TREASURES

Like a broken record, two scenes played over and over in my mind.

In the first scene, I'm standing outside the New Jersey warehouse three months after moving back to America. Movers are unloading our sea crate from East Asia and piling our boxes and furniture in a truck headed to Florida. I stare down at the jewelry box I'm holding, wrapped inconspicuously in a couple of plastic grocery bags. I pause to consider keeping it with me, but instead, I hand it to the mover? Or do I? Maybe I lay it down in the parking lot? In the midst of the chaos, it's a fog.

When we unpacked the truck in Florida, it was gone.

Each time I thought of it, I kicked myself. *Why, why, why didn't I keep it with me?? If only I had kept it with me! What a stupid thing to do.*

Peter called the warehouse, the truck company, and the movers, to ask if perhaps my jewelry box ended up in lost and found. Of course, no one said they had seen it.

I gained some satisfaction imagining the pawnshop clerk laughing hysterically as the suspected thief tried to trade my jewelry for cash. "This stuff?" The pawnbroker wrinkles his nose. "This isn't even worth a dollar!"

Anyone who may have stolen that box was not going to get rich off of my cheap trinkets. But to me, they were all priceless, and I was caught off-guard by the depth of grief I experienced. The contents of the box contained priceless memories of treasured people and events from our ten years overseas.

It is the value the owner gives an object that determines its true worth.

The second scene that kept playing over and over in my mind was how I imagined I would like to see this story end. It went like this: I am sorting through our storage boxes when suddenly, somehow, I discover my jewelry box. I can't believe it's true! I tear into the bag, throw open the jewelry box, and scream for joy!

This imagined happy ending spurred me on. Several times I frantically searched through our boxes and luggage, with hope against hope that my fantasized conclusion would happen.

But it didn't.

Days turned into weeks, weeks into months. I surrendered the fate of my treasured box into His Hands. Little by little, He softened the sharp pain into a dull ache.

Several months later, we picked up our Christmas decorations at the storage unit. As I straightened up the boxes from our sea crate, something caught my eye. Then...I couldn't believe my eyes! There was my jewelry box's familiar blue-flowered pattern peeking through a plastic bag. Here was that happy ending, exactly as I had imagined.

As I carefully caressed each piece of jewelry, I relived those special moments when I received them. I felt moved as my friend gave me the earrings she wore at her wedding. I once again stood gawking at the sparkling bracelets at the Asian marketplace, on our first trip there. I was pushed along by the jostle of the crowds and smelled the roasted sweet potatoes on

Hong Kong's vendor-lined street, then I ducked into a souvenir shop for those beautiful decorative pins. I remembered the thrill of my birthstone necklace, a surprise from Peter after his first trip to Thailand.

I cried deep tears of joy. What a wonderful gift had been returned to me! I stood in awe that what once was lost now was found.

The Lord gives...and the Lord takes away.

And sometimes the Lord gives back.

I was flabbergasted that God had heard my heartfelt cries and somehow returned my treasures. He is not a harsh God, anxious to grab away the things we hold dear. He delights in lavishing His blessings on us more than we love to receive them.

I have absolutely no idea how my jewelry box got there, or how we could have overlooked it when we searched several times through our storage unit. But I have no doubt my loving Father knew all along that the happy conclusion I imagined would come true. Those months when I wondered where my jewelry had been scattered, it was locked up in a safe place. Perhaps sometimes He allows us to lose what we cherish so we can receive a greater prize: a clearer glimpse into how much He values us and those not yet in His safekeeping.

As I grieved my loss during those months of searching, I began to understand how the Lord feels about His lost treasures, each and every human being on the planet earth. He feels deeper grief over one person who has not been brought into His family than I could ever experience. I am comforted in knowing the loved ones I grieve over and am praying for are His lost treasures. He will never stop seeking them and inviting them to Himself. Never.

For those who know Jesus, this is a beautiful picture of what it means to belong to Him. In the world's eyes, we may feel we are just a piece of worthless costume jewelry. But to the One to whom we belong—the One who decides our true value—we are each His priceless treasure. He feels indescribable joy when we come to Him, like I felt as I lovingly examined each of my cherished baubles.

That's what being treasured is all about.

To reflect:

Have you ever lost something valuable to you? What did you do in response to that loss?

To consider:

Or suppose a woman has ten silver coins and loses one. Doesn't she light a lamp, sweep the house and search carefully until she finds it? And when she finds it, she calls her friends and neighbors together and says, "Rejoice with me; I have found my lost coin." In the same way, I tell you, there is rejoicing in the presence of the angels of God over one sinner who repents. Luke 15:8-10 NIV

According to these verses, how valuable are you to God?

52

TRAGEDY ON THE BEACH

It started out as the perfect day for a relaxed walk on the beach...until it took a sudden unexpected turn.
    I smiled as I watched carefree children charging into the waves while mothers in beach chairs sipped drinks under strategically angled, well-placed beach umbrellas. Teens with headphones applied sunscreen to their already-burned shoulders. Men in baseball caps with determined faces flung their fishing lines in again, buckets ready for the big catch. The warmth of the sun and the gentle breeze lulled me into a peaceful mood. All was well with the world.

Until I saw it.

Up ahead, several paramedics were running across the sand toward what I now realized was someone lying on the sand. A few workers were already frantically pumping the man's chest over and over again. I stood praying for this man, the medical staff, and his loved ones.

Others gathered around, respectfully keeping their distance, and a middle-aged couple holding the victim's dog described to me what happened. They had been watching absentmindedly as the man hurried into the water to retrieve his pet. He looked like he was playing when he fell sideways into the waves, got up, and wobbled sideways again. They were alarmed when he didn't get up the third time, and called 911.

After twenty minutes of trying to revive him, they carried him away on a stretcher. There were indications he most likely was gone, but they continued futilely pumping his chest. A young woman standing close by went with them, leaving the dog with strangers.

Was she his girlfriend? Wife? Daughter? Is she replaying the scene over and over again in her mind? What were their last words to each other? Had they argued about who would go into the water to retrieve the dog, and now she is flooded with regrets? Or had he chivalrously offered to go in after the dog, his final heroic act being her lingering memory?

Two chairs and a beach umbrella stood conspicuously abandoned in the sand; two drink glasses sat half-empty on a cute little table between them. They silently shouted the fragility of life, which most of us seldom think about. One minute, he had been basking in the sun with his companion, enjoying his favorite drink. The next minute, he was dead.

Just like that.

My heart was heavy as I walked away. It was sobering to be reminded that every day—every minute—is a gift from God and could be our last.

Had this man trusted Jesus for eternal life? Was he in heaven or separated forever from everything good? What would he have done differently if he had known it was his last day on earth? What would she have done differently?

Only a few yards down the beach, people were oblivious to the drama that had just unfolded. Delighted children still splashed in the waves while their moms talked, teens laughed, and fishermen concentrated on their fishing lines. They had no idea what had just happened a few steps away.

The sunset that evening was beyond spectacular. The deep

reds spread across the sky in a way only a master artist like God could create. I drank in its beauty with a deeper appreciation of all He has given us to enjoy on this earth, as I remembered we are just passing through. Sadness overshadowed my awe, as I couldn't stop thinking about the man who would never see another sunset.

When I got back home, I hugged Peter a little longer. And I was thankful. Thankful that whether our time ends suddenly or we have advance notice, we can be certain of a far better place after death. Sin afflicts every human being and results in one hundred percent death. Jesus guarantees a never-fail, universal cure for the disease of sin. It's free for the asking.

What would you do differently today if you knew it was your last day? Or the last day of someone you love?

One of these days, it will be.

To reflect:
If this were the last day of your life, would you do anything differently?

To consider:
You have made my life no longer than the width of my hand. My entire lifetime is just a moment to you; at best, each of us is but a breath. Psalm 39:5 NLT

What are your thoughts about life after death?

53

HOME!

With my backpack tightly gripped and feet poised for a split-second take-off, I didn't listen to a word my fourth-grade teacher said. I didn't want to miss the end-of-school bell, as I envisioned capturing the ultimate prize: the front seat of the bus.

My classroom on the third floor offered a distinct disadvantage. I had tried before, unsuccessfully, to beat those who were conveniently located on the lower floors. But today would be different. Today I would out-run and out-jump all of them and claim my reward.

The bell had not even finished buzzing, and I shot out the door like lightning. Picking up speed on the first flight of stairs, I raced toward my goal. I leapt over the last five steps leading down to the second floor, to keep my momentum. After sailing weightlessly through the air for a few seconds, I crumpled in a heap as my foot bent sideways with a crack.

Stunned by the pain, I slowly picked myself up and hobbled down the remaining two and a half flights of stairs. I was pushed to the back of the crowded bus just as it began to pull away.

Bracing myself on one foot as we lurched forward, I bravely hid my physical and emotional agony. Not only had I missed out on the coveted front seat, but I had to stand on my injured foot for the long ride home. Not a tear was shed along the way. *Who would care?*

After what seemed like an eternity, it was finally my stop. Gingerly stepping down the tall bus steps, I stoically limped several blocks along the dirt shoulder of the road toward home.

But the second I walked through the door and saw my mother's face, I collapsed into a tempest of tears. Safely wrapped in her arms, I dropped my brave mask. I no longer needed to pretend to be strong or hide my brokenness. I was with someone who loved me, so I could be a hurting little girl who desperately needed someone to comfort me.

I was home. I was home!

That was long ago, and I have fallen into the "Valley of the Broken" many times since. I've experienced broken hopes and dreams for myself, my life, marriage, and children. Wounds of the soul and the spirit don't heal as neat and tidy as young bones do.

At times, I've felt like that helpless girl crumpled on the floor again, wondering how to pick myself up. Or someone I love has collapsed and, as much as I might try, I can't control their decisions or the outcome.

I still have the tendency to try to be strong, forcing myself forward by sheer determination. If I just work harder and longer, I will reach the proverbial front seat.

Helping others can be a way to ignore my pain and unmet needs. God gently reminds me that I don't always need to be the one offering comfort and strength. Just as I was able to run into my mother's arms and pour out my pain, I can run into my Heavenly Father's arms. I can unashamedly be a hurting, needy little girl who desires someone to take care of her.

One day when life felt especially overwhelming, the image

of being embraced in my mother's arms came to mind. But this time, it was Jesus' arms. For just a few seconds, everything weighing on my shoulders was lifted. I wasn't thinking about the next thing I had to do, worrying about my children, or wondering what the future would bring. Just absolute stillness in my soul.

I have tried, unsuccessfully, to recreate that scene and its tranquility. I think it was a foretaste of what life will be like beyond the grave. Jesus will have written the last chapters of my story, and will tenderly scoop up my spirit to be with Him forever.

Upon leaving this world, anyone who accepted Jesus' gift of eternal life will be ushered to His heavenly home. We will have absolutely no stress, no nagging regrets, no to-do list. There will be no worries, no fears, no hurt feelings. Just perfect peace in His welcoming arms.

No brokenness of any kind. Everything that was broken in this world will then be made whole. Completely and forever.

Revelation 21:4 seems to say that when we first meet Him face to face, He will tenderly wipe away the tears remaining from our sorrows on earth. After that, there will be no more crying as we enjoy His perfect love for all eternity.

We will be home. We will be home!

To reflect:
Imagine for a minute what it would be like to have no death or mourning or pain. Which of those things would you most like to be free from?

To consider:
He will wipe every tear from their eyes. There will be no more death or mourning or crying or pain, for the old order of things has passed away. Revelation 21:4 NIV

Do you have the assurance you will be "home" in Jesus's arms, when you pass from this life to the next?

WOULD YOU LIKE TO JOIN THE JOURNEY?

GOOD NEWS

Maybe you have read my stories and are thinking, "I could trust a God like that!" Well, there's good news!

Here are the four simple principles from the Bible that two women shared with me many years ago in the college cafeteria. These truths explain how you can begin a personal relationship with God through Jesus Christ.

PRINCIPLE 1
God loves you and offers a wonderful plan for your life.

GOD'S LOVE
"God so loved the world that He gave His one and only Son, that whoever believes in Him shall not perish, but have eternal life" (John 3:16).

GOD'S PLAN
Jesus said, "I came that they might have life, and might have it abundantly" (John 10:10) — that is, that life might be full and meaningful.

Why is it that most people are not experiencing the abundant life? Because ...

PRINCIPLE 2
All of us sin, and our sin has separated us from God.

WE ARE SINFUL
"All have sinned and fall short of the glory of God" (Romans 3:23).

We were created to have fellowship with God, but because of our stubborn self-will, we chose to go our own way, and our fellowship with God was broken. This self-will, characterized by an attitude of active rebellion or passive indifference, is what the Bible calls sin.

WE ARE SEPARATED
"The wages of sin is death" (Romans 6:23). Death is spiritual separation from God.

This image illustrates that God is holy and people are sinful. A great gulf separates us. We are continually trying to reach God and the abundant life through our own efforts, such as a good life, philosophy, or religion – but we inevitably fail.

The third principle explains the only way to bridge this gulf ...

PRINCIPLE 3
Jesus Christ is God's only provision for our sin.

Through Him we can know and experience God's love and plan for our lives.

HE DIED IN OUR PLACE
"God demonstrates His own love toward us, in that while we were yet sinners, Christ died for us" (Romans 5:8).

HE ROSE FROM THE DEAD
"Christ died for our sins ... He was buried ... He was raised on the third day, according to the Scriptures ... He appeared to Peter, then to the twelve. After that He appeared to more than five hundred." (1 Corinthians 15:3-6).

HE IS THE ONLY WAY TO GOD

"Jesus said to him, 'I am the way, and the truth, and the life; no one comes to the Father, but through Me'" (John 14:6).

God has bridged the gulf that separates us from Him by sending His Son, Jesus Christ, to die on the cross in our place to pay the penalty for our sins.

It is not enough just to know these three principles ...

PRINCIPLE 4
We must individually receive Jesus Christ as Savior and Lord; then we can know and experience God's love and plan for our lives.

WE MUST RECEIVE CHRIST

"As many as received Him, to them He gave the right to become children of God, even to those who believe in His name" (John 1:12).

WE RECEIVE CHRIST THROUGH FAITH

"By grace you have been saved through faith; and that not of yourselves, it is the gift of God; not as a result of works, that no one should boast" (Ephesians 2:8-9).

When we receive Christ, we experience a new birth.

WE RECEIVE CHRIST BY PERSONAL INVITATION

Jesus says, "Behold, I stand at the door and knock; if any one hears My voice and opens the door, I will come in to him" (Revelation 3:20).

Receiving Christ involves turning to God from self (repentance) and trusting Christ to come into our lives to forgive our sins and to make us what He wants us to be. Just to agree intellectually that Jesus Christ is the Son of God and that He died on the cross for your sins is not enough. Nor is it enough to have an emotional experience. You receive Jesus Christ by faith, as an act of the will.

Principals

Which circle would you like to have represent your life?

SELF-DIRECTED LIFE

You may be a good person and try to do the right things, and pray. Or you may not have thought much about God before reading this book. Or you might have deliberately done things you knew were wrong.

The one thing all of these have in common is that they are directing their life and trusting their own efforts. You have not yet asked Him to come into your life, to forgive your sins, and make you the person He created you to be.

CHRIST-DIRECTED LIFE

Your life is not perfect. But at some point in your life, as an act of the will, you asked Jesus to come into your life, forgive your sins, and make you the person He created you to be. You have the promise of eternal life and a personal relationship with Him.

You can receive Christ right now by faith through prayer.
Prayer is talking to God. God knows your heart and is not so concerned with your words as He is with the attitude of your heart.

The following is a suggested prayer. If this prayer expresses the desire of your heart, then you can pray this prayer right now and Christ will come into your life, as He promised.

"Lord Jesus, I need You. Thank You for dying on the cross for my sins. I open the door of my life and receive You as my Savior and Lord. Thank You for forgiving my sins and giving me eternal life. Take control of the throne of my life. Make me the kind of person You want me to be. "

Does this prayer express the desire of your heart?
If it does, you can pray it right now and Jesus will come into your life as He promised.

NOTHING WOULD THRILL NANCY MORE

Nothing would thrill Nancy more than to hear from you! If you have a question about anything in her book or have a story of your own to share, please email her at Tiretracksfromgod@gmail.com

Check out Nancy's website at nancybeverlyauthor.com

Also by Nancy Beverly

Available June 1, 2025!

Adventure. What is it?

Is it for the daring few who boldly jump into death-defying feats while the rest of us watch in awe from the sidelines? Or is an incredible adventure waiting for each of us, including the shy, the fearful, the hesitant?

Ask Nancy; she's an unlikely adventurer herself.

In her second award-winning book, Nancy's true stories will inspire and guide you to that "something more" you have been missing. In the process, you will be drawn closer to the Great Adventurer Himself, Jesus.

Don't wait another day to discover your great adventure!

Also by Nancy Beverly

Available in simplified Chinese

柏兰馨
NANCY BEVERLY 柏兰馨

轮 胎 印 记
TIRE TRACKS

亲历上帝的信实：生命实录
TRUE STORIES OF A FAITHFUL GOD

ACKNOWLEDGMENTS

With deep sincere gratitude to:

First and foremost, Jesus: The One who replaced my emptiness with song and gave me a life story worth sharing.

Maggie Bruehl, for believing in me when I didn't believe in myself; and for her tireless and invaluable editing and encouragement. This book may not have happened without her help!

Richard and Helen Ward, for walking alongside us in many ways, including the generous use of their beach condo where these stories began to come to life.

Linda LaScala, Judy Douglass, Dr. Shepson, Steve, and others for their very helpful editing.

Our loyal team of ministry partners, who have shown us the kindness and generosity of God. Their partnership has eternally impacted us and those we have ministered to.

Our faithful online prayer group, whose prayers have paved the way for us through many a spiritual jungle.

All my Word Weavers friends, who have encouraged me and refined my writing skills.

ABOUT THE AUTHOR: NANCY BEVERLY

Little did this cautious, small-town girl know the adventures that lay ahead when she asked Jesus to come into her life. Being squirted with a water hose in 1973 was the unlikely catalyst for her spiritual journey.

Since then, Nancy has traveled to 26 countries. She has seen penguins in Africa, kangaroos in Australia, sunsets in Thailand, and Big Ben in London. She was kissed by a camel in Israel and has danced with locals in Turkey. She has struggled at times with doubts and despair.

Her most meaningful adventure has been knowing the God of the universe and seeing Him do amazing things only He could do. This includes Jesus changing people's lives all over the world.

Nancy loves bike riding, jazzercise, gardening, walking and talking with her husband, deep conversations, and of course anything with her adult children and grandchildren.

Made in the USA
Columbia, SC
20 March 2025